Christian Orthodoxy
in the Second Century

Christian Orthodoxy
in the Second Century

How Did the Early Church Anchor Her Faith
After the New Testament?

MICHAEL JIN CHOI

Foreword by Donald Fairbairn

RESOURCE *Publications* • Eugene, Oregon

CHRISTIAN ORTHODOXY IN THE SECOND CENTURY
How Did the Early Church Anchor Her Faith After the New Testament?

Copyright © 2024 Michael Jin Choi. All rights reserved. Except for brief quotations in critical publications or reviews, no part of this book may be reproduced in any manner without prior written permission from the publisher. Write: Permissions, Wipf and Stock Publishers, 199 W. 8th Ave., Suite 3, Eugene, OR 97401.

Resource Publications
An Imprint of Wipf and Stock Publishers
199 W. 8th Ave., Suite 3
Eugene, OR 97401

www.wipfandstock.com

PAPERBACK ISBN: 979-8-3852-3702-9
HARDCOVER ISBN: 979-8-3852-3703-6
EBOOK ISBN: 979-8-3852-3704-3

12/30/24

"Scripture quotations are from the ESV® Bible (The Holy Bible, English Standard Version®), © 2001 by Crossway, a publishing ministry of Good News Publishers. Used by permission. All rights reserved. The ESV text may not be quoted in any publication made available to the public by a Creative Commons license. The ESV may not be translated in whole or in part into any other language."

This book is dedicated to

My wife, Priscilla, who has been
the blessed loving friend in this journey,

and to our son, Paul,
who has been that constant joy to his father.

Contents

Foreword by Donald Fairbairn | *ix*

Preface | *xiii*

Acknowledgements | *xv*

Abbreviations | *xvi*

CHALLENGES TO CHRISTIAN ORTHODOXY AFTER THE NEW TESTAMENT

1   The Critical Discontinuity from Judaism | 3
2   The Gnostic Imagination | 22

THE GOSPEL AS THE CENTER OF CHRISTIAN ORTHODOXY

1   The Creation | 49
2   The Fall | 62
3   The Redemption | 77
4   The Consummation | 93

Bibliography | *109*

Foreword

IN THE HISTORY OF Christian thought, the second century is possibly the most important time outside of the New Testament period itself. It was during the second century that the Christian church learned to cope with the loss of the apostles while still waiting expectantly for the return of the Savior. That century saw the church's most important and long-lasting efforts to establish its identity in contrast to both the Judaism that had birthed it and the hodgepodge of Greco-Roman mystical and philosophical ideas—labeled with the catch-all term "Gnosticism"—that surrounded it. The second century saw the acceptance of the documents of the new covenant alongside those of the old, and thus the beginnings of what would later be called the New Testament canon. The second century saw the emergence of distinctly Christian worship practices—born out of the worship of the Jewish synagogue but re-cast in light of the crucifixion and resurrection of Christ. By the end of that century, a form of Christianity such as we envision it today—what came to be called "normative" Christianity or "historic Christian orthodoxy"—was clearly present and recognizable.

But the importance of second-century Christianity is not limited to its historical position. It also stands as an entity that is profoundly relevant to us in the twenty-first century, precisely because the world second-century Christians encountered was so surprisingly similar to our own. Of course, the pace of technological innovation today outstrips the entire previous history of mankind, but the world of the Eastern Hemisphere in the early

Foreword

Christian centuries was no stranger to innovation either. Its road systems—from Spain to China—and ease of communication were unprecedented in human history and would never be equaled again until well into the modern period. The proliferation and importance of written texts rose dramatically as a result of a new way of publishing books, the codex, that enabled longer writings to be bound together and read easily. (Most notably, the entire New Testament could fit into a single codex/book.) The religious ferment that was present—as polytheism was challenged by versions of pantheism and even by true monotheism—rivalled anything we find today in the exchange of religious ideas.

Even more particularly, the Mediterranean world in the second century was haunted by the same spiritual ghost that lingers over western civilization today—Gnosticism. This set of loosely related religions was highly individualistic, focusing on the ability and responsibility of each person to recognize the divine spark within himself, to actualize his own divinity. The key to such self-realization was a body of secret knowledge—a set of passwords, if you will—that Jesus supposedly communicated orally to his disciples and that bypassed the hard road of the cross, humility, and repentance in favor of the more congenial spiritual pathway of discovering oneself to be both divine and the center of all things. Gnosticism even bent the idea of gender in ways that anticipated recent developments in western culture. If these ideas sound eerily familiar, they should. Gnosticism is still with us today, and it is even in ascendancy in certain pseudo-academic circles in the western world.

With the ascendancy of a new Gnosticism today has come a remarkable effort to re-write the history of early Christianity. In the hands of contemporary scholars—men and women who by their own admission are no fans of the way of the cross and who transparently long for a "Christianity" that doesn't rely on sin and redemption—historic Christian orthodoxy has been turned into only one "Christianity" among many, one option on the religious smorgasbord that a person then or now could choose to satisfy his own spiritual longing. Many scholars now tell us that

Foreword

there were other options out there, other "Christianities" basing their teachings on different Bibles than ours, understanding different ways to salvation, and even believing in different numbers of gods. Moreover, these scholars tell us that the "Christianity" that eventually won out was victorious mainly by chance and political circumstance, not because there was anything inherently true about it. This new story—pushed aggressively for a century now by modern scholars—stands as a dramatic counter to the church's longstanding story of its own history, in which a common faith (historic Christian orthodoxy) was held by most, challenged by a few (the heretics), and refuted by the great thinkers of Christianity (the church fathers).

But this new story put forward by contemporary scholars tends to founder on the rocks set out by the second century's greatest theologian (indeed, the Christian church first true theologian), Irenaeus of Lyons. Irenaeus was a Greek-speaking easterner who spent his adult life in the far west of the Christian world, in Lyons in what is today southeastern France. There he suffered for the faith in two major persecutions (ca. 177–78, and again ca. 202–3), probably losing his life in the second of those. There he meticulously studied the great heresies that had emerged as contrasts to historic Christian orthodoxy and wrote (ca. 180) a monumental work that we call *Against Heresies*. In this work, Irenaeus lays out the teachings of the Gnostics so accurately that even today's scholars grudgingly admit that he understood them very well, and the scholars take their own summaries of Gnosticism from Irenaeus as much as from the Gnostic writings themselves. In this work, Irenaeus also puts forward a grand positive vision of the Christian faith, of God's work with humanity from creation to final resurrection, and he contrasts this vision poignantly with the varied conceptions of the Gnostics.

Irenaeus' vision of Christianity is biblical. He quotes thousands of times from both the Old Testament and the emerging New Testament, and he describes God's work with the human race in a nuanced way. His vision is comprehensive. It includes both the objectivity of legal forgiveness of guilt and the warmth of adoption as sons, while attending to the salvation of both the soul and the body in the midst of "Christian" heresies that belittled the physical. His vision is relevant. It addresses concerns and issues that have resurfaced in our world recently. Michael Choi's little book walks the reader through both the context and the content of Irenaeus' teaching, providing a panoramic overview of the understanding of Christianity that the early church would regard as normative. This vision is one that will both reassure contemporary readers (as we see that the faith as we understand it has a long and distinguished pedigree) and challenge us (as we grasp connections and implications of our faith that we might have forgotten). I commend Choi's overview to readers today who want to dip their toes into the world of the second century and into the thought of its greatest Christian thinker.

Donald Fairbairn
Robert E. Cooley Professor of Early Christianity
Gordon-Conwell Theological Seminary

Preface

WHY A BOOK ON Christian orthodoxy in the second century? Since theological orthodoxy is always developed in the face of challenges posed by the questions from the past tradition as well as the contemporary culture, a short answer is 'to understand the history of doctrinal development in that period.' More pointedly, our aim is particularly to examine the sources from the perspective of how the gospel, the centerpiece of Christianity, withstood the rigorous challenges of heterodoxy, and what theological insights could be discovered from this debate between the view held by mainstream Christianity, 'the great church' as Origen calls it, and the differing interpretations of this new revelation in Christ.

One might also ask 'Why during the second century?' This has a simpler answer. By the end of the second century students of history are able to 'get the picture' of whether or not the church was able to compellingly respond to these various questions and novel interpretations that were heavily entrenched in a worldview conflicting with the biblical worldview.

The first section will identify the core doctrines of Christianity as they conflicted with two major cultures or traditions, namely Judaism and Gnosticism. On the one hand, the earliest Christian community since the Pentecost event was still rooted in the Old Testament, but she also needed to distinguish herself from Judaism in light of the teachings of Christ and of the Apostles. This is the topic addressed by Justin Martyr which is observed in the first chapter, 'The Discontinuity from Judaism.' On the other hand, this new-found identity of the church had attracted many intellectual questions from her contemporary Graeco-Roman culture. And the most vexing problem faced by the church during that period was Gnosticism. This is addressed by our reading of two documents *Against Heresies* and *Epistula Apostolorum* in the second chapter, 'The Gnostic Imagination.'

The second section outlines the Christian worldview in the simplest way by presenting the four epochs according to the events of the divine economy—the creation, the fall, the redemption, and the consummation. This four-fold scheme of redemptive history not only corresponds to Irenaeus' understanding of the biblical narrative reflected in the 'rule of faith,' but it also summarizes the gospel, the restoration of all creation through Christ. The church's affirmation of these four areas of doctrine bring unity of the Old and New Testaments, and therefore unity to the divine purpose of the gospel, the redemption and restoration in Christ. Indeed, the problems and challenges of Christian thought in any segment of church history have no exact parallels in the theology of the Early Church, but the gospel is the centerpiece of Christian orthodoxy, the form of Christianity that would endure into the present evangelical churches today, even as Paul testifies, 'I delivered to you as of first importance what I also received: that Christ died for our sins in accordance with the Scriptures, that he was buried, that he was raised on the third day in accordance with the Scriptures, (1 Cor. 15:3–4).

Each of these four chapters, then, is a reflection on the expositions given by Irenaeus in his two extant writings, *Against Heresies* and the *Apostolic Preaching*. Each one is an attempt to remember how Irenaeus sought to mount a counteroffensive against the gnostic misinterpretation by presenting the gospel in the second century for transforming individuals and churches of ancient civilization.

Michael Choi
Professor of Systematic Theology
Torch Trinity Graduate University

Acknowledgements

IN PREPARING THIS BOOK the seminal ideas began to take shape in Belgium, where I have benefitted greatly through many encouragements from my colleagues Gie Vleugels, Martin Webber, and Jack Barentsen, who have made it enjoyable and worthwhile for me to be part of the Research Center for Early Christianity at Evangelische Theologische Faculteit (ETF). I am indebted to Donald Fairbairn for writing such a helpful foreword. I am also grateful to Wipf & Stock Publishers who agreed to publish this important volume.

The author gratefully acknowledges permission to reprint the following material: "What is Christian orthodoxy according to Justin's Dialogue?" *Scottish Journal of Theology.* 2010; 63(4) 398–413. © Scottish Journal of Theology Ltd 2010 - DOI: https://doi.org/10.1017/S0036930610000487; "Cerinthus for Gnostic Survival According to Irenaeus and *Epistula Apostolorum.*" *Journal of the History Society in Korea* 36 (2013) 11–46; "Creation in the Development of the Human Person According to Irenaeus," *Torch Trinity Journal* 14 (2011) 120–129; "Irenaeus on Adam's Sin." *Expository Times* 130, no. 12 (2019) 521–529; "Irenaeus on Law and Justification." *Expository Times* 130, no. 2 (2018) 53–61.

Abbreviations

1–2 Apol.	1–2 Apologies
Ad Eph.	Ad Ephesians
AH	Against Heresies.
ANF	The Ante-Nicene Fathers
ATR	Anglican Theological Review
C.Cel.	Contra Celsus
CCSG	Corpus Christianorum Series Graeca
Epid.	Epideixis
Eth.Nic.	Nicomacean ethics
Leg.	Legatio Pro Christianis
GNO	Gregorii Nysseni Opera
HTR	The Harvard Theological Review
JBL	Journal of Biblical Literature
JECS	Journal of Early Christian Studies
JEH	Journal of Ecclesiastical History
JRH	Journal of Religious History
JTS	Journal of Theological Studies
NHL	Nag Hammadi Library
NPNF	The Nicene and Post-Nicene Fathers

Abbreviations

NTS	*New Testament Studies*
Or. Dom.	*Oratio Dominica*
PG	*Patrologia Graeca*
PTS	Patristische Texte und Studien
QG	*Quaestiones et solutiones in Genesin*
SC	Sources Chrétiennes
SNT	*Supplements to Novum Testamentum*
SP	*Studia Patristica*
ST	*Studia Theologica*
TDNT	*Theological Dictionary of the New Testament*
TU	Texte und Untersuchungen
VC	*Vigiliae Christianae*
ZAC	*Zeitschrift Für Antikes Christentum*

CHALLENGES TO CHRISTIAN ORTHODOXY
AFTER THE NEW TESTAMENT

1

The Critical Discontinuity from Judaism

IT HAS BECOME COMMONPLACE to revise early Christian literature particularly from socio-political studies. One of the more vigorous recent contributions to this cause is by Daniel Boyarin,[1] whose claims any scholar in the field of Jewish–Christian relations is now hard-pressed to ignore.[2] Boyarin makes the claim that the binitarian view of God was common to Jews and Jesus-followers until the time of Justin. Given this situation, Justin aimed to construct, by writing the *Dialogue*, a self-definition of Christianity over against Judaism so that the latter would have a portrayal which denies belief in the Logos.[3] The rabbis, thereafter, we are told, began to respond to this ground-breaking Christian religious identity by

---

1. Boyarin, *Border Lines: The Partition of Judaeo-Christianity*.

2. See Paget, Review of *Border Lines*, 338–41, and more recently, Dunn, Review of *Border Lines*, 229–33.

3. Boyarin, *Border Lines*, 146, says, "I suggest that an important motivation for Justin's expenditure of discursive energy is not so much to convince the Jews to accept the Logos, but rather to deny the Logos to the Jews, to take it away from them, in order for it to be the major theological center of Christianity, with the goal of establishing a religious identity for the believers in Christ that would, precisely, mark them off as religiously different from Jews."

naming the archetypal idea of "two powers in heaven" a heresy within Judaism. Boyarin summarizes thus:

> The Dialogue, by establishing a binary opposition between the Christian and the Jew over the question of the Logos, accomplishes two purposes at once. First, it articulates Christian identity as theological. Christians are those people who believe in the Logos; Jews cannot, then, believe in the Logos. Second, Christians are those people who believe in the Logos; those who do not are not Christians but heretics . . . If Christian identity is theological, then orthodoxy must be at the very center of its articulation, and for Justin belief in the Logos as a second divine person is the touchstone of that center, the very core of his religion.[4]

These are some provocative claims, yet any given theory must also be put to the test in relation to the text in question. And if Boyarin is right, as I think he is, to identify the area of christology as the matrix of the *Dialogue*[5] for Justin's definition and defense of Christianity, closely re-examining these christological texts is imperative. The purpose of this article, then, is to see what Justin really emphasized as the touchstone of Christian orthodoxy in writing this treatise. Rather than selecting a few passages from the text to support a socio-political theory about Justin's possible motive behind the text, I should like to evaluate the central message of the *Dialogue* from the viewpoint of structural analysis with special reference to Justin's major assertions and claims about Jesus Christ. Is the existence of the Logos as another God the central thrust and thesis of this treatise? This affirmation of the pre-existent Logos is significant for Justin, but I hope to show from the overall design of the text that it remains subsidiary to the most compelling doctrine about Christ, namely, the crucifixion of the Messiah, one that was truly responsible for sealing the "parting of the ways."

First, a reasonable outline of the *Dialogue* is necessary in order to situate significant text(s) on Justin's christology into the

---

4. Ibid., 39.
5. See also Skarsaune, *The Proof from Prophecy*.

context of the entire treatise. My fundamental assumption for the proposed outline below is based on two complementary elements with reference to both christological and non-christological themes found in the text itself. At *Dialogue* (henceforth *D*) 45.1 we are told that (1) there is a "predetermined order" of various topics in the debate and (2) there are interruptions, asides and repetitions which Justin judiciously entertains throughout.[6] Thus, by eliminating obvious and subtle digressions which occur between Justin and Trypho while tracing the continuity of christological themes, we can delineate Justin's more focused discourse on his christology, supported by extensive scriptural proof-texts and exegesis. Once the basic outline helps to gain a synthetic account of Justin's structural arrangement of his ideas about Christ, a commentary on each of Justin's multiple categories about Christ will follow, and along the way fresh light may be shed. But all of this will be subordinate to the chief objective of this article – to determine the epicenter of Christian orthodoxy in the *Dialogue* by ascertaining which aspect of Christ receives the greatest emphasis in the text.

A THEMATIC OUTLINE OF THE DIALOGUE (D)

I begin, then, with an outline of the *Dialogue*, with particular attention to Justin's discourse about the life and works of Christ. These may be divided into three major parts aside from the prologue:[7]
Prologue: Philosophical inquiry (*D* 1–9)

I. *Preliminaries* (*D* 10–54)
 Ritual laws of the Old Covenant (10–30)
 The coming of the Messiah (31–4)
 More ritual laws (35)

---

6. Quotations from Justin are taken from Marcovich's critical edition of *Dialogus cum Tryphone*. Translations are my own.

7. Apart from the prologue (1–9), the thematic groupings into three parts are generally similar although their boundaries are disputed. Skarsaune, *Proof*, divides them into 11–47, 48–108 and 109–42; Marcovich, PTS 47, gives the following division: 10–47, 48–108 and 109–42.

Various prophecies, symbols and types about the Messiah (36–44)
Mosaic Law superseded by the New Law (45–7)
Two comings of Elijah (48–54)

II. *The Life and Works of Christ* (D 55–108)
"Another God" (55–62)
Christ was virginally born (63–78)
[Rabbinic changes on the LXX texts (72–4)]
Christ will come as Judge over all creatures (79–83)
[Christian vs. rabbinic interpretations of some passages (83–4)]
[Prophecies repeated for second-day listeners (85)]
Christ was crucified for our sake (86, 89–108)
[Gifts of the Holy Spirit (87–8)]

III. *Reprise and Exhortation* (D 109–42)
The call of the Gentiles (109)
Summary of arguments (110–14)
The Gentiles as new Israel (115–25)
Christ's many names according to function (126–9)
Reproach to the Jews (130–6)
A final plea to turn (137–41)
Farewell (142)

Early in part I Justin introduces the Christ of the scriptures as the "only sure and profitable philosophy" (*D* 1–9) and matters of ritual laws of the Old Covenant as preliminaries in comparison to topics directly relating to Christ. Eliminating and responding to Trypho's more immediate objections such as those concerning circumcision, Sabbath and ritual laws (*D* 10–30), before resuming the main discussion, is Justin's manner of debate with Trypho (*D* 45.1). Thus these preliminaries come around to the coming of the Messiah (*D* 31–4), only to be drawn aside again about dietary laws superseded by Christ the New Law (*D* 35–47).[8] Trypho then proceeds to ask about Christ's pre-existence and deity, but also objects that Jesus

---

8. See Marcovich, *Dialogus*, 36.

The Critical Discontinuity from Judaism

could not be the Messiah since Elijah must first come; again Justin ends up addressing here only the last of these three in any substantial way (*D* 48–54).

In the second and middle part we encounter Justin's formal proof about Jesus' identity as Messiah (*D* 55–108). These important chapters probably form the core of the treatise, and display in four general categories the life of Christ in chronological order, except for one. Thus, they are the pre-existent (*D* 55–62), incarnate (*D* 63–78), ascended Christ (*D* 79–83), before culminating in his last topic on this subject of the identity of Christ—the crucifixion (*D* 89–106).

The third and last part naturally follows part two as Justin brings forth his missionary message, namely that Christ the crucified calls for repentance and faith. Justin recapitulates the previous arguments (*D* 110–14, 126–9) while paying special attention to God's calling of the Gentiles and their response of faith in Jesus (*D* 109, 115–25, 130–6). Justin sets this schema against the blindness of the Jewish teachers (*D* 137–41) hoping to provoke his listeners to jealousy and repentance.

THE LIFE AND WORKS OF CHRIST

At the beginning of the *Dialogue* Justin laments that most philosophers neglect to ask two critical questions: "whether there is one or plurality of gods, and whether they have a regard for each one of us" (*D* 1.4). The first of the following four categories about the identity of Christ (i.e. "another God") is concerned with the former question, while the last three (i.e. incarnation, judgement and crucifixion of Christ) relate to the latter one. To grasp just how Justin conveys his central concern to Trypho in this text, one can hardly do better than first to examine the thrust of his arguments in each of the four categories. In doing so, I should like to explain why the last of the four (i.e. the crucifixion of Christ) is the most important and thereby the central message of Justin in writing his *Dialogue*.

Challenges to Christian Orthodoxy After the New Testament

"Another God" (D 55–62)

Justin answers in three ways Trypho's request (D 50.1) for proof of the existence of "another God": that he was given the divine name, shares a divine substance and also participated as Creator. First, Justin demonstrates[9] that one other than the Father appeared to Abraham (D 56.4), Jacob (D 58.3, 9, 10) and Moses (D 59).[10] He also elaborates, though briefly, on the nature of Christ using metaphysical categories. While the theological vocabulary for articulating the ontology of the Son's relationship with the Father is evidently limited during Justin's time, he elaborates that the nature of this unity is grounded in the fact that he was begotten of the Father (D 61). The two analogies—human utterance of a word and the enkindling of a fire—are used to stress the distinct identity of the divine Persons, but also the unity of substance shared between them. The Son is "begotten (*gegennesthai*) from the Father . . . but not by abscission (*apotome*) as if the substance (*ousia*) of the Father has been divided . . . [And this] enkindled fire is distinct from that [original fire], from which many can be kindled is by no means diminished (*elassoo*)."[11] Beyond this, Justin cites Proverbs 8:21–36 without any commentary bearing upon matters such as how the Son was begotten or the mode of his existence prior to his

---

9. Justin takes up here Trypho's challenge to demonstrate that Jesus is not reverenced as another one of the numerous deities of the Gentiles. Indeed, Justin shows awareness of Dionysus, Herakles, Alcmene (D 69.1–3, 70) and Simon (1 *Apol.* 26); and he asserts the unique identity of Christ as not only different from them, but also as one who received worship by Abraham, Jacob, and Moses.

10. Unlike Origen who reserved *ho theos* only to designate the Father, Justin employs *ho theos* as well as *theos* in reference to Christ; this is true even when Justin is not citing scripture. See esp. D 56.10 and 59.3 in our present section, but also 61.3 and 113.4.

11. D 128.4; at D 61.2 Justin uses the same illustration of the utterance of a word, but at D 128.3–4 it is significant that his response to the false teaching that angels were the result of some emanation from the Father is given in the same context in which he is refuting the false teaching on the identity of the Son; thus Justin indicates that the Son, though called an Angel, is to be clearly set apart from all actual angels who do not come from the "substance" of the Father.

The Critical Discontinuity from Judaism

generation.[12] Nonetheless, he is clearly asserting on the one hand Christ's distinction from the Father without division or separation, but also by implication on the other hand, Christ's unity with the Father by virtue of the same divine substance they share.

Now, one might ask even more to the point: "Does Justin attempt to communicate this sharing of the divine substance without any metaphoric analogy?" In fact he does. This is to be found in the use of the word *gnome* (mind) in his brief but explicit assertion about the unity of the Father and the Son:

> He who is said to have appeared to Abraham, and to Jacob, and to Moses, and who is called and written down as God, is different from the God who made all things numerically, I say, but not in mind (*gnome*). For I say that he has never at any time done anything which he who made the world – above whom there is no other God – has not wished him both to do and to engage himself with. (*D* 56.11; Marcovich, 163)[13]

The word *gnome* had a variety of meanings among the philosophers during Justin's time, and its use in the *Dialogue* is also diverse enough to include four basic categories denoting "opinion" (*D* 1.6; 35.4; 35.6; 39.1; 68.8), "disposition" (*D* 44.1; 47.2), "will" as in "purpose" (*D* 56.12; 95.2; 125.4) and, finally, "mind" as in the "organ by which one perceives or knows" (*D* 56.11; 93.4; 127.4).[14] Only the last category, as cited above, refers to the faculty out of which the first three operations ensue.[15] For early evidences of *gnome* as combining the notion of "intellect" and "will" we could go back to Heraclitus who defines wisdom thus: "to understand

---

12. Cf. *D* 62.4; Osborn, *Justin Martyr*, 29, notes that Justin differentiates between "offspring *gennemata* and things made *poiemata* pointing to the priority of the former."

13. The unity of thought and will between the Father and the Son finds fuller expression among the Cappadocians in their defense of the Trinity based on the same operation of the Persons, e.g. cf. Gregory of Nyssa, GNO III,1.43–4.

14. Liddell et al., *A Greek-English Lexicon*, "gnome."

15. Justin makes even clearer at *D* 93.4 this distinction of *gnome* as a *faculty* rather than its product as in *opinion*.

gnome (intelligence) that guides everything in every way" (fr. 41), but later, Aristotle also defined *gnome* as the faculty which helps one to judge righteously in society.[16] Christian precedents are noted in which the word was similarly applied to God; for instance, believers are exhorted "to perceive . . . the *gnome* (mind) of the goodness of our Father" in the *Epistle of Barnabas* (2.9). But, most significantly, Justin's use of the word for the relationship between the Father and the Son is clearly reminiscent of Ignatius whose idea of unified divine purpose and thought is explicit: "For even Jesus Christ our inseparable life is the mind (*gnome*) of the Father . . ."[17] Moreover, since Homer, the notion of the mind or will of Zeus was often "the Master Mind" representing the will of a plurality of gods expressing the unified divine purpose.[18] Juxtaposing this idea current in his day, it is likely, then, that Justin uses the concept of divine purpose to express the organic unity between the Father and the Son, so that the Father is the source of deity and the Son an outflow from the Father: they have the same mind (*gnome*) (*D* 56.11) or substance (*ousia*) (*D* 128.4).

Having shown the divine name for Christ and explicated how the Father's divine substance is shared by the Son, Justin moves on to another aspect of Christ's deity, his participation in the Father's act of creation, a topic that follows naturally from Proverbs 8 he just cited. Since his most frequent title for God the Father is the "creator of all things" or "creator of the world,"[19] it is not surprising that reference to the Son's involvement in creation is limited to a few instances in the *Dialogue*.[20] At *D* 61, however, Justin's ex-

---

16. *Eth.Nic.* 6.11.

17. *Ad Eph.* 3.2. Justin's contemporary Athengoras, while using different terms, combines this dual idea of intelligence and volition for the unity between the Father and the Son (*Leg.* 10.2): "But the Son of God is the Logos of the Father, in idea and in operation (*en idea kai energeia*)." For further developments up to Maximus the Confessor, see Lampe, *Patristic Greek Lexicon*, 317–78.

18. See West, "Towards Monotheism," 23–4.

19. *D* 7.3; 16.4; 35.5; 38.2; 48.2; 55.1, 2; 56.1, 4, 10, 14, 23; 57.3; 60.2, 3; 67.6; 102.6; 116.3; 117.5; 34.7; 56.3, 16; 58.1; 60.2, 3; 68.3; 84.2.

20. Later, when Justin cites Ps 96:1–13, Trypho objects that it refers to the

The Critical Discontinuity from Judaism

egesis focuses on the account of the creation of man in Genesis 1:26–8 and specifically points to the plurality of the expression "Let us make" to assert Christ's involvement in creation (*D* 62.2). Although he does not take pains to speak of the Holy Spirit,[21] perhaps for reasons of simple apologetics, he merely says that there are revealed *at least* (*elaschistos*) two in number in the expression "as one of us" in Genesis 3:22 (*D* 62.3; Marcovich, 177). He rejects an interpretation by a Jewish heretical sect,[22] or any other which maintains that the Father was speaking to angels, or that the angel was responsible for the creation of man's physical body. As Skarsaune notes, Justin's polemic is possibly directed here against Tannaitic and Philonic interpretations.[23]

Now if Justin is aware of the writings of Philo, which Boyarin adduces as one of the key points of evidence that most Jews were binitarians, perhaps a more nuanced explanation for Justin's charge against the Jewish teachers' unbelief concerning the Logos could be expressed in a two-fold way – as a lack of specificity and therefore also of certitude. As Boyarin recognizes,[24] the uniqueness of Christianity was in identifying the Messiah in the particular person Jesus. This same logic can be applied to Jewish teachers'

Father (*D* 74.1). But Justin replies that the Holy Spirit exhorts people to "recognize that he is to be praised and feared, and that he is the maker of heaven and earth (*poietes tou te ouranou kai tes ges*), who effected this salvation in behalf of the human race, who also dying after he was crucified, and was deemed worthy by him [the Father] to reign over all the earth" (*D* 74.3; Marcovich, 198). Outside the *Dialogue* an explicit reference to Christ as participating in creating everything is found in 2 *Apol*. 6.

21. The lack of triadic formulations in this treatise and esp. of *D* 68.3 seems to present a binitarian view; but adducing proof for the deity of the Holy Spirit would compound the apologetic task for Justin. Also, Stanton, "The Spirit in the Writings of Justin Martyr," 331, persuasively notes: "When one considers all the references to the Spirit in the *Apology* . . . Justin attaches considerable importance to earlier Christian traditions and shows himself to be heir (however indirectly) to triadic passages such as Matt 28:19 and 2 Cor 13.14."

22. Danielou, *The Theology of Jewish Christianity*, 68, suggests that Justin has in mind a Jewish heterodoxy related to Cerinthus, who taught that the world was created by angels.

23. Skarsaune, *Proof*, 389, n. 31.

24. Boyarin, *Border Lines*, 105.

Challenges to Christian Orthodoxy After the New Testament

understanding of Logos' identity as well. While the hermeneutic role of the Logos/Torah, i.e. for interpreting scriptures, may have been generally emphasized in Judaism, this Logos has not been sufficiently and specifically identified with a particular person[25] in the Jewish scriptures (e.g. as one who appeared to the patriarchs, *D* 56–62); certainly, Philo pointed to the plurality in "let us create . . ." (Gen. 1:26) or "as one of us . . ." (Gen. 3:22) as a reference not to the Logos, but rather to "unspeakable number of powers" (*Opif.* 24; *Conf.* 33–4).[26] As such, what Justin calls "the mystery of Christ in the scriptures," i.e. the notion of connecting the Logos precisely with the coming Messiah, would be even more difficult to believe. Wherever specificity is absent, any belief would remain little more than tentative speculation at best.

Christ was virginally born (D 63–78)

Trypho is actually convinced of (*D* 60.3), and admits that Justin has proved his point on, the existence of another God:

> And Trypho said, "Friend, you have proved this point forcibly, and through many arguments. Finally, then, prove also that he submitted according to the will of his Father to become man by the virgin, and to be crucified, and to die. Prove clearly also that after this he rose again and ascended into heaven." (*D* 63.1)[27]

---

25. Philo calls logos *ton deuteron theon* only once (*QG* 2.62); however, it is disputed among scholars whether Philo clearly spoke of the Logos as a divine hypostasis. As Runia, *Philo in Early Christian Literature*, 41, notes, "the Logos . . . in Philo's thought may be described as that aspect of God which is turned toward creation." For a similar judgement of Philonic logos as "merely an aspect" see Weiss, *Untersuchungen zur Kosmologie*, 320. For the difference between Philo's logos and Justin's logos, see esp. Barnard, *Justin Martyr*, 92–6.

26. In this vein, Rokéah, *Justin Martyr and the Jews*, 27, notes BT Sanhedrin 38b reporting a debate in which a Jewish Christian claims that Gen 1:26, 11:7 and 19:24 refer to two gods. Here, R. Ishmael b. R. Jose's denial is based on a sermon given by R. Meir, who is a contemporary of Justin and a prominent supporter of the Bar Kokhba Revolt. Admittedly, the record is anachronistically noted, yet its historical veracity cannot be completely ruled out.

27. Also, Skarsaune, "Is Christianity Monotheistic?", 357–58, remarks, "On

The Critical Discontinuity from Judaism

Now, Trypho is also challenging Justin for evidence concerning three other claims about the life of Christ which he perceives to be more difficult to believe; they are virginal birth, crucifixion and ascension. Justin complies with the first and the last respectively but reserves the topic on the crucifixion until the end.

From a list of various passages from the Psalms and the prophets cited by Justin, it was Isaiah 7:10-17 that advances Justin into a long debate with Trypho when the latter protests on three different grounds: (1) the text says "young woman" not a "virgin," (2) the whole prophecy refers to Hezekiah, not to Christ, and (3) any story of a virginal birth is as mythical as the story of Perseus born of Danae (*D* 67.1-2). Although Justin has periodically to pull himself up to resume his argument, he takes these three objections and responds to them one at a time in reverse order (*D* 69-70, 77-8 and 84).

This extensive discussion on the birth of Jesus, continued over to the second day,[28] is clearly a segment where worship of Christ is treated in the most emphatic way. First, this is intimated because among a variety of terms used for worship,[29] Justin's favorite

---

this point, and on this point only, [Trypho] declares himself fully convinced."

28. Prigent, *Justin et l'Ancien Testament*, 212 ff., thinks that the Isaiah materials in *D* 63, 66-7 and 77-8 were together in Justin's source.

29. While in his *Apologies*, *therapeia* (1.9 and 1.12) and *thereskeuo* (1.62) are two other terms used to denote worship or service, Justin limits himself to three different terms and their derivatives to express the idea of worship in the *Dialogue*: *sebomai*, *latreuo* and *proskuneo*. Based on his high regard for the LXX (*D* 68.7, 71.1, 84.3), Justin is probably following the LXX usage on the meaning of each of these terms: *sebomai* (15 occurrences in the entire *Dialogue*), and its derived form *theosebeia* "worship of God" is used most widely in the context of general piety to God. It is noteworthy that Justin reserves this word only for God the Father or the Son and never to idols or demons. Moreover, different forms of *latreuo* (23 occurrences in the *Dialogue*), which also denotes cultic worship of the God of Israel, are directed either to God or Christ; on the other hand, Justin's most frequent use of this term is the derivative form, *eidololatreuo*, when he has demons/idols as objects. But clearly his most frequent term is *proskuneo* occurring more than the other two words combined (41 occurrences in the *Dialogue*). He also takes its sense in the usual LXX terminology for worship of the true or false God. He narrowly designates this term and all of its derivative forms to indicate worship either to a true

word *proskuneo* as worship to Christ is more densely employed here than elsewhere in the entire *Dialogue*: more than half of all forms of *proskuneo* as references to Christ are found in this small section which constitutes only about one tenth of the book.[30] Second, the context of *D* 63–78 for the argument of Christ's virginal birth parallels Justin's emphasis on the worship due Christ. Justin opens with this theme on worship due to Christ (*D* 63) and closes with the assertion that indeed Christ, even as a babe, had been rightfully worshipped by some (*D* 78). We can also easily trace in these chapters how Trypho's series of different objections (*D* 64, 65, 69–70, 71–3, 74 and 77) were triggered by Justin's pressing the issue every so often that Christ must be worshipped (*D* 63.5; 64.1; 68.3).

Christ will come as judge over all creatures (D 79–83)

What began as Trypho's angry reaction to Justin's assertion that even angels have sinned leads into a discussion about the end of the world and the role of Christ as the judge over all creatures including angels. Further, Trypho's incredulity about the rebuilding of Jerusalem and joyful gathering of all the saints around Christ (*D* 80.1) allows Justin to re-engage on the topic concerning the expectation of the Messiah (*D* 31–4). This time, however, he is able to develop the theme of Christ as judge in an extended way within the context of a more comprehensive eschatological discourse, still grounded in his schema of the two comings mentioned earlier (*D* 34.2; 39.7). Accordingly, the humiliated Son in the first coming does not yet possess his eternal kingdom, but the exalted Son who has overcome all humiliation of his earthly life[31] shares with the

---

God, i.e. the Father and the Son, or to false gods, idols and demons. Greeven, "*proskuneo*," *TDNT* 6:758, notes: "Almost three-quarters of the instances of *proskunein* in the LXX relate to veneration and worship of the true God and Lord or to that of false gods." Cf. Acts 10:25–6; Rev 19:10; 22:9.

30. Of the 29 *proskuneo* references to Christ in the *Dialogue*, 17 references are used here.

31. *D* 32.2; Trakatellis, *The Pre-existence of Christ in the Writings of Justin*, identifies this idea of reversal as the lynchpin of Christology for all of Justin's

The Critical Discontinuity from Judaism

Father this divine sovereignty over all creation. This idea is best depicted through Psalm 110 which he cites again here.

In the previous discourse that relates Christ as the eschatological judge (*D* 31–9), Justin had explained the phrase "Sit at my right hand" (Ps. 110:1) as pointing particularly to the resurrection of Christ (*D* 32.3). Upon Justin's further elaboration with passages from Daniel 7 and other psalms, Trypho concedes that these prophecies concerning his coming again are all foretold in the scriptures (*D* 39.7). Yet, Trypho reiterates the gist of his objection, namely, against Justin's claim that none other than this *crucified* Jesus[32] is the Messiah spoken of in the scriptures. To the Jewish interlocutor's request for further proof Justin consents and promises to comply, but at a more proper place (*prosekonti topo*).[33] Our section *D* 79–83, then, seems to be Justin's keeping, at least in part, his earlier promise.

The *duo parousiai* schema[34] (*D* 110.2), therefore, is the basis for Justin's second attempt to prove the identity of the one sitting at the right hand of the Father (Ps. 110:1); this he endeavors within the context of a comprehensive discourse concerning the end of the world recorded in *D* 79–83. He speaks about fallen angels (*D* 79), the millennium and the resurrection (*D* 80–1), judgement of unbelievers (*D* 82) and culminates with the identity of the one who "sits at the right hand of the Father" (*D* 83). If we compare his comments here on Psalm 110 (*D* 83) with his earlier ones (*D* 32–3), two differences are evident. First, in the earlier account, Christ is called "Lord," and "Lord Jesus Christ," whereas, in the

---

extant works.

32. See *D* 32.1 and 38.1.

33. A similar postponement of a reply to Trypho until a more fitting place occurs in 36.2. This method seems to help organize an otherwise more disorderly arrangement apparent in the *Dialogue*.

34. Stanton, "The Two Parousias of Christ," 194, notes: "In Matthew, Justin and Origen, the two parousias schema is a response to the sharp criticisms of Jewish opponents who insisted that Christian claims about the Davidic Messiahship of Jesus were not in accordance with the prophets." As Skarsaune, *Proof*, 285, notes, the New Testament uses *parousia* for the Second Coming only, but Ignatius is the first to use the term for Christ's earthly life.

latter, he is simply named "Jesus" and "Christ" (*D* 83.4). Second, and this seems related to the first, Justin, notwithstanding his longer citation (Ps. 110:1–7), is satisfied to merely bring out the idea of Christ's resurrection in the earlier account: "the Father of all led him up from the earth . . . after his rising (*anastasis*) from the dead" (*D* 32.3; Marcovich, 122). In the latter account, where he cites fewer verses (1–4), Justin adds comment on the phrase "sent forth a rod (*hrabdos*) of power into Jerusalem" (Ps. 110:2): "though he has not yet come in glory, this phrase signifies the word of calling and of repentance" (*D* 83.4; Marcovich, 214). The significance of this change from the earlier account is twofold: (1) Justin first took the opportunity to stress Christ's exaltation in order to easily connect with the more prevalent Jewish expectation of the Messiah; but after further demonstration with other prophetic passages, Trypho must now be ready also to deal with the burden of new evidence that Christ is the judge to whom accountability of our lives must be given. (2) Christ is not just another judge who comes in power, but one who calls or *invites* repentance by his "provisionary" rod. This is Justin's important play on the words "rod of power" as signifying both the judgment and the cross. This he amply demonstrates in the following section (*D* 86) where he explicitly says Christ's "return in glory after the crucifixion was prefigured by the tree," the rod of Moses, of Jacob, of Aaron, of David and of others. In this section, then, Justin's *kerygmatic* zeal presents Christ the apocalyptic judge and the provider of redemption calling forth repentance.

Christ was crucified for the whole human race (D 89–106)

After listening to extensive arguments on the virginal birth and the second coming of the Messiah, Trypho admits that all the scriptural quotations Justin has adduced indeed refer to Christ. Nevertheless, there is still one other unresolved objection which Trypho expresses as his real point of doubt, that "Christ should be so shamefully (*atimos*) crucified" (*D* 89.2; Marcovich, 225).

The Critical Discontinuity from Judaism

As it is Justin's pattern to first remove his listeners' most immediate and obvious objection (*D* 45.1; 68.9), he attends to the problem that crucifixion is a curse according to the Mosaic law (Deut. 21:23) before providing an extensive commentary on Psalm 22. Justin's solution is based on what he has explained earlier concerning the scriptures, that some commandments are intended for worshipping God and practicing righteousness, but some are given for the purpose of "the mystery of Christ" (*D* 44.2). Moses' making the brazen serpent should have been a clear indicator, Justin argues, that this incident is not to be interpreted only literally. The obvious paradoxical nature of God's command that goes against his own command not to make any graven image bespeaks that it is no ordinary event but one that clearly belongs in the category of "the mystery of Christ." And if the mystery of Christ is signified here, Justin asserts that it points specifically to the crucifixion, as he painstakingly demonstrates from numerous prophecies (*D* 40.1; 43.3; 74.3; 86.6; 91.1–3; 91.4; 94.2–4; 97.4; 106.1; 107.1; 115.1–116.1; 125.3–5; 131.2; 134.5; 138.1–3).

This leads us to a significant observation that Justin points to the cross on each of these fifteen Old Testament passages (out of the eighteen in the *Dialogue*) which he explicitly identifies as pertaining to the mystery of Christ.[35] In fact, this is the case even when the passages are generally cited as proof-texts for the pre-existent Logos (*D* 43.3; 125.3–5). Several other textual pointers can be offered as evidence for our claim that crucifixion is central to the *Dialogue*. First, the crucifixion of Christ is also by far the longest and most uninterrupted section on a single topic in the *Dialogue*. Second, the crucifixion has been the most troublesome aspect of Christ to his interlocutor. It is contrary to Trypho's idea of hope (*D* 10.3), opposed to his concept of the honorable and glorious Messiah (*D* 32.1), and that this crucified one is claimed to have conversed with Moses and Aaron in the pillar of clouds is

---

35. Here, we only refer to passages which Justin labels *musterion*. Other symbols and types of the cross are also enumerated, e.g. in *D* 86. Three other "mystery of Christ" passages refer to the virginal birth (*D* 68.6), Christian's new birth (*D* 85.7) and Christ's calling of believers from every race (*D* 139).

nothing less than blasphemy (*D* 38.1). Even after acknowledging that the Messiah would suffer (*D* 89.2), the mere thought of attributing this shameful manner of death accursed by the law was unbearable to Trypho (*D* 90.1). Third, as previously noted, Trypho had requested as evidence concerning the claims about the life of Christ, i.e. his "virginal birth, crucifixion, and ascension," in this chronological order (*D* 63.1). Significantly, Justin, despite his own arrangement of the categories so far, which reflects the chronology of the life of Christ from his pre-existent state, breaks away from this natural sequence in the life of Christ. In the light of his usual pedagogic/apologetic reasons, Justin delays the topic of the greatest challenge for his interlocutor, Christ's shameful crucifixion.[36]

One other forceful evidence has to do with Justin's understanding of both the exclusive and the inclusive nature of salvation on account of the crucifixion. This can be seen in his repeated assertions that the Messiah was crucified for *all* who would believe in him. Thus, even in regard to social behavior, Trypho is puzzled how "setting hope in the crucified man" (*D* 10.3) can cause Christians to expect to be approved by God in their non-segregating inclusive attitude towards non-Christians.[37] Just as he has been attributing the fall into the serpent's deceit as the origin of human sin and evil in the Genesis account (*D* 79.4; 88.4; 91.4), Justin makes it unambiguous that the mystery of Christ in the brazen serpent incident proclaims the breaking of the same serpent which incited the sin of Adam (*D* 94.2). The bite of the serpent in the wilderness, therefore, is not merely a picture of the predicament faced by the

---

36. In fact, the entire section on the identity of Christ thus far (*D* 55–83) followed the chronological order of the life of the Son, beginning from the pre-existent state to the virgin birth and ending with the millennium, except the crucifixion. Thereafter, we have a recapitulation for second-day listeners (*D* 84–8) before proceeding to the last topic, the crucifixion; clearly Justin seems to delay it as the climax of the debate.

37. Boyarin, *Border Lines*, 38, mistakenly takes this passage to be Justin's confession via Trypho's mouth of his personal "identity crisis." This interpretation would seriously distort the meaning of the context because Justin immediately answers (*D* 11.1–2) that this precise charge of disregarding ritual segregation is now nullified.

The Critical Discontinuity from Judaism

Jews but of how sin entered the human race through Adam. For Justin, the effect of sin is universal:

> And indeed every race of men will be found to be under the curse, being thus according to the Law of Moses: For "cursed," it is said, "is everyone who does not remain in all things that are written in the book of the Law to do them." And no one ever did all exactly – you will not dare deny this – but some have observed the commands more and some less than others. But if they who are under this law are manifest to be under a curse, because they did not observe everything, how much more shall all the Gentiles be shown as being under a curse, who even serve idols, and seduce youths, and all other evil works? (D 95.1)

No one is excluded from the bites of the serpent, but no one, Justin asserts, needs to be excluded from Christ's salvation either, for Christ "proclaimed salvation to those who believe on him . . . to save them from the bites of the serpent" (D 94.2). Certainly his polemic against the Jews is obvious in the *Dialogue*, but equally evident are his untiring pleas and exhortations to believe in Christ by repentance (D 35.8; 44; 53.4; 64.3; 92.6; 95.3; 108.3; 118.1; 120.2; 25.1–2; 130.2; 133.1, 6; 134.4; 136.1; 137.2; 138; 139.5; 141.1; 142.2), affirming that God knows that "every day some of you are becoming disciples in the name of Christ, and leaving behind the way of error" (D 39.3).[38] Justin believes that only the crucified Christ who invites all to believe is the most inclusive means of salvation from the universal curse of sin, and so he is also prompted to say to Trypho that "there is no other way" (D 44.4).

This inclusive soteriology has been Justin's heartbeat and conviction from the start. As we have seen, Justin delineated for us a criterion at the beginning of the *Dialogue* for evaluating a good philosophy by asking two questions: whether there is one or more

---

38. In fact, this salvation, inclusive of the Jews, is further demonstrated in Justin's positive reply to Trypho's query whether a believer in Christ but also an observer of Mosaic Law would be saved (D 47.1–4). The only injunction is that the person in question does not, out of his fervor for the Old Law, become someone who denies Christ and dies without repentance (D 47.4).

gods, and whether they care for each one of us (*D* 1.4). We have also seen that only the first category, that there is "another God," concerns the former question, while the last three categories relate to the latter question. This emphasis on the salvific providence is already foreshadowed in the remainder of this first chapter (*D* 1.4–6) through Justin's utter concern for one's destiny in the afterlife, lamenting that most philosophers were "neither fearing punishment nor hoping any benefit from God" (*D* 1.5). It is in response to this remark that Trypho then invites Justin to explain his personal view on this subject (*D* 1.6–2.1). After relating his conversion story, Justin claims that Christianity is exclusive on the one hand, since he "found it alone to be the sure and profitable philosophy" (*D* 8.1), but inclusive, since everyone including the Jews is also invited to personally have "regard for [one]self, care about, and eagerly seek salvation" (*D* 8.2).

CONCLUSION

Although we can appreciate much of Boyarin's creative analysis, his charge that Justin's *Dialogue* was an attempt to construct Judaism contrary to what it was cannot be maintained. First, a gross misrepresentation would only undermine Justin's own credibility to his contemporary readers. Moreover, contrary to Boyarin's claim that for Justin belief in the Logos is the very touchstone of Christian orthodoxy, that this is what defines and divides Christianity from Judaism is not reflected by our close reading of the text. As we have seen, Justin finds this belief in another God the easiest way to convince his interlocutor, and he must go on to demonstrate something of greater magnitude, though more troubling it may be for Trypho. According to Justin, it was not just the "second God" but the "incarnate God," and even more emphatically, the crucifixion of this incarnate Messiah which is the epicenter of Christianity, which also happens to be the main stumbling block for the Jews. In the final analysis, Justin demonstrates faithfulness, at the least, to what he had been bequeathed by the apostles, this very salvific truth claim of blood redemption in the crucified Messiah.

The Critical Discontinuity from Judaism

Much of what I have tried to show is related to a concern about an overdependence on the theory of hybridity,[39] a method of socio-political analysis perhaps helpful for understanding cultural and ethnic identities, but reductionistic for grasping the religious phenomenon of conversion. If Boyarin were to discuss this matter with Justin, one can imagine that Boyarin would agree that the incarnation (although he tries to find some compatibility even here), and certainly, the particular identity of Jesus as the incarnate crucified Messiah, is a novum for Judaism. And quite obviously Boyarin would disagree with Justin's estimation that most of the Jews were non-binitarians during Justin's time. Now it is certainly easy to focus the discussion on the matters upon a new disagreement (i.e. whether most Jews were binitarians), rather than on the matters upon which one already agreed to disagree (i.e. belief in the incarnation, and especially the particularity of the crucified one). It appears, however, that this natural tendency to gravitate towards the point of new disagreement has misled Boyarin to think that precisely this new disagreement must also define orthodox Christianity for Justin. Nevertheless, if Justin were given a chance to reply, he would again disagree. For Justin, the belief in "another God" would simply continue to be Judaism if this Logos was never enfleshed and crucified.

---

39. This catchy term for describing the fluid nature of one's mixed "situatedness" first gained prominence in ethnic and postcolonial studies (Bhabha, *The Location of Culture*), and its concept continues to be in flux.

2

The Gnostic Imagination

ON THE RECENT STATUS on the study of ancient Gnostic religion study, Majella Franzmann remark is revealing:

> It is difficult to believe that, as recently as 1990, the New Testament scholar Robert Grant could write: "In spite of the exciting and valuable Gnostic documents recovered from Nag Hammadi in Egypt, the basic starting point for the study of the Gnostics has to lie in the earliest criticisms by Christians who wrote against heretics." Scholars believe the rhetoric, the propaganda of the winners that they have read for so long. They believe the history from the mainstream Christian group which holds only the canonical scriptures and their interpretation of them as the true basis of what historically a Christian and Christianity meant so that all other early systems or alternate systems must be judged in their light. Why should the paradigm of one Christian group be axiomatic for the history and analysis of the entire movement?[1]

Scholarship on the Gnostics is still clearly polarized, depending on one's basic assumptions whether one takes it along with Irenaeus, for instance, to be a Christian heresy, or whether one assumes that it is independent and/or antecedent to Christianity.

---

1. Franzmann, "A Complete History of Early Christianity," 117-28.

The Gnostic Imagination

From the socio-ethical perspective, as Franzmann objects, "the paradigm of one Christian group [should not] be axiomatic for the history and analysis of another movement or religion." But it would be improper historiography if we neglect the fact that portions of *Against Heresies* by Irenaeus concerning these Gnostics also stand attested as reliable by other independent sources including the *Apocryphon of John* in the Nag Hammadi Library. In this article, therefore, building upon recent research that has placed Irenaeus' account on a firmer footing than was previously recognized, I shall survey an independent document, the *Epistula Apostolorum,* to examine how this data converge with Irenaeus' account, especially on Cerinthus. Based on these analyses, I propose that it was Cerinthus who had implemented the most decisive adaptation for its staying power, by locating the doctrinal focus of his system to his version of, but nevertheless the familiar New Testament themes of, Christ as redeemer and the resurrection. In this sense, Cerinthus, due to his partial dependence on the canonical scriptures, was the key person responsible for supplying a major Gnostic reconstruction—a "theological leverage" as it were—that successfully fortified an enduring Gnostic salvation myth suitable to be further innovated by Gnostic leaders like Saturninus and others. Finally, I shall give a survey of how modern Gnostic documents currently being produced also provide some level of confirmation for this proposal.

WHY BEGIN WITH IRENAEUS?

Is it truly unjustifiable to begin with Irenaeus? One could mention Michael Williams's famous book, *Rethinking Gnosticism*, in which he argues that Irenaeus is not trying to show us what "gnosticism" is but what *heresy* is.[2] He concludes that one should, therefore, not try to study these Gnostic sects by beginning with Irenaeus' catalogue. Williams's first assertion holds true in the light of the fact

---

2. Williams, *Rethinking "Gnosticism,"* 45.

Challenges to Christian Orthodoxy After the New Testament

that "Gnosticism" is a seventeenth-century historian's construct;[3] yet, his conclusion does not necessarily follow. In fact, even his first assertion seems to require a more nuanced explanation because Irenaeus' use of the label "the Gnostics" varies from a general to a more particular notion.[4] Indeed, Irenaeus sometimes uses the expression "knowledge falsely so-called" broadly to include various opposing heresies referring explicitly to Paul's coinage in 1 Timothy 6:20 (*AH* 2. pref. 1). Nevertheless, there are also instances where the label seems to more narrowly identify particular doctrines of a specific group such as the school of Valentinus (e.g., *AH* 1.11.1). And finally, it is not very clear in some passages in *AH*.[5] Be that as it may, Williams' complaint that Irenaeus' term is dubious cannot be exaggerated to say that one should not begin with Irenaeus' catalogue for studying these Gnostic sects. Even if we were to use Williams' proposed category "biblical-demiurgical traditions"—which is already predisposed to Williams's own definition—there is no compelling reason not to use Irenaeus' account as the starting point, especially when Irenaeus provides the *earliest* extended account of these Gnostics at our disposal.[6] In other words, other first and second century "sects" or non-orthodox groups are mentioned here and there in the bishop's account; yet, Irenaeus clearly intended to write from his own historical vantage point a loosely-tied family tree of "sects" which happen to predominantly share a certain set of traits such as cosmological

---

3. Layton, "Prolegomena to the Study of Ancient Gnosticism," 348-49, argues that the term was first coined by the Cambridge Platonist Henry More in 1699.

4. Haar, *Simon Magus*, 231, correctly points out *AH* 1.29.1; 2.13.10; 3.11.2; 4.33.3.

5. *AH* 2.13.8-10; 2.31.1; 2.35.2; 3.4.3; 3.10.4; 4.6.4; 4.35.1, etc. See Haar, *Simon Magus*, 231. Cf. Markschies, *Gnosis*, 1-27, for a detailed treatment of the strengths and weaknesses of respective arguments for different uses of the term *gnostikos*.

6. From an etymological side, Haar, *Simon Magus*, 230, properly points out that while the term *gnostikos* was applied to one's mental facility or aspects of a personality since the fourth century BCE, it was never applied to individuals until the second century CE, and thus signifies a major innovation by Irenaeus.

The Gnostic Imagination

dualism,[7] biblical-demiurge, and salvific self-knowledge when compared to many more kinds of "sects" that emerged throughout history. And when Irenaeus takes the freedom to mention a non-biblical-demiurgical sect, he does this to disclose the origin of a particular error, especially when it is repeated in many other related sects that are so-called "biblical-demiurgical traditions."

A loosely-tied family tree of "sects" does not mean, as Karen L. King argues, that Irenaeus presents Simon as the first heretic by merely depending on family genealogy as a powerful rhetorical metaphor that "drew upon notions of biological reproduction to naturalize the socially constructed view that 'like produces like.'"[8] While she asserts that "It is genealogy, not a common content, that continues to justify all these varied persons, groups," other scholars like Beyschlag Karlmann and Gerd Lüdemann properly point out that according to *AH* 1.23-28 most heterodox positions have "at least one detail of what Simon had already taught."[9] This is not to say that every Gnostic teacher was related to Simon in such a way as if each element of his teaching must be genetically traceable to him. Irenaeus is much more nuanced to perceive that the Gnostics were generally embracing two disparate impulses at the same time: an independent spirit for innovation as well as a certain thread of continuity. In one place Irenaeus differentiates the orthodox succession of bishops from his opponents, indicating that the latter distinguish themselves as extreme individualists who will freely adapt to or break away even from other Gnostic teachers, which would be in keeping with their refusal to follow Scripture or tradition (*AH* 3.2-3). Yet, as we shall see, Irenaeus also recognized that the evolution of the Gnostic religion could be organized loosely by categories of certain shared doctrines as these heresiarchs were developing their system.

---

7. An important distinction is made between ethical dualism of the fourth Gospel (and of the Qumran community) and cosmological dualism of the Gnostics by Charlesworth, "A Critical Comparison of the Dualism," 389-418.

8. King, *What is Gnosticism?*, 31-32.

9. Lüdemann, *Heretics*, 19, follows Beyschlag, *Simon Magus und die christliche Gnosis*, 16. n. 19 and 141. n. 24.

Challenges to Christian Orthodoxy After the New Testament

A SOURCE BEHIND IRENAEUS

In the last third part of Book 1 of *AH*, Irenaeus outlines the "family tree," as it were, of the Valentinian heresy introduced earlier in the first part of the book. One of the puzzling aspects, however, of his accounts of the heresiarchs is the arrangement. While Irenaeus starts with Simon Magus, who is identified as the one "from whom all sorts of heresies derive their origin" (*AH* 1.23.2), the list in *AH* 1.23-27 is not merely chronologically, but also doctrinally enumerated, because it seems to broadly group distinct doctrines, albeit not without variations propounded by the founder of each sect. The precise reason for ordering the list was not immediately evident. Recently, however, Charles E. Hill made a convincing case for identifying the source of these groupings as well as the order in which they are given.[10] Following Frederick Wisse's lead that Irenaeus must have had access to some catalogue of heresies later than Justin's,[11] Hill identifies a passage in Irenaeus' fourth book of *AH* as an important clue to Irenaeus' source for an even *earlier* catalogue than Justin's:

> After this fashion also did a presbyter, a disciple of the Apostles reason with respect to the two testaments, proving that both were truly from one and the same God. For [he maintained] that there was no other God besides Him who made and fashioned us, and that the discourse of those men has no foundation who affirm that this world of ours was made either by *angels, or by a certain power* (*quamlibet virtutem*), *or by another God*. (*AH* 4.32.1; PG 7A:1070B; italics are mine)

Hill argues that this presbyter is most likely Polycarp of Smyrna, who rejected three different types of heresies which correspond with Irenaeus' three distinct categories in the earlier catalogue in *AH* 1.23-27, and that both accounts are given in the same order.[12]

---

10. Hill, "Cerinthus, Gnostic or Chiliast?," 135-72.

11. Cf. Wisse, "The Nag Hammadi Library and the Heresiologists," 214-16.

12. See his recent monograph on this premise, *From the lost teaching of Polycarp*. Accordingly, the doctrine of creation by "angels" identifies the first

CERINTHUS—JEWISH AND GNOSTIC

Before we unravel Cerinthus' role as the innovator of a firmer Gnostic soteriology, perhaps it is helpful to briefly recap the debate about his identity, a common misunderstanding which I believe has been cleared up only recently. The bishop's description of what Cerinthus believed in summary fashion in *AH* 1.26.1 will be discussed later. The difficulty, however, has to do with *how* we should interpret Irenaeus' presentation of the Ebionites along with Cerinthus in the second text:

> Those who are called Ebionites agree that the world was made by God; but their opinions with respect to the Lord are similar to those of Cerinthus and Carpocrates (*ea autem quae sunt erga Dominium non similiter ut Cerinthus et Carpocrates opinantur*). They use the Gospel according to Matthew only, and repudiate the Apostle Paul, maintaining that he was an apostate from the law. As to the prophetical writings, they endeavor to expound them in a somewhat singular manner: they practice circumcision, persevere in the observance of those customs which are enjoined by the law, and are so Judaic in their

---

group (Simonian, Menandrian, Basilidean, Satornilian, Carpocratian); the doctrine of creation by "certain power" belongs to the Cerinthians; and by "some other God" point to Cerdonians and Marcionites. While it cannot be assumed with certainty that Polycarp is the presbyter as Hill asserts, the three distinct categories here furnish us with the most likely reason for Irenaeus' peculiar ordering of the list in *AH* 1.23-27. Moreover, Irenaeus' implication of a level of authority here by identifying the source as a "disciple of the apostles" might also strengthen this argument. On the other hand, if Irenaeus is trying to ascribe authority by means of this phrase, it seems unlikely that he would conceal Polycarp's identity, especially when earlier he chose to name Polycarp as the witness to John's encounter with Cerinthus at the bath house (*AH* 3.3.4), unless the presbyter was not a very prominent figure. Nonetheless, it is possible that Irenaeus is unsure of the exact identity of his source other than that he was a disciple of the Apostles especially if he is dependent on an oral tradition. Thus Polycarp cannot be ruled out, but the source would be at least a contemporary of Polycarp, and if we believe Irenaeus, the catalogue of the early heresiarchs in *AH* 1.23-27 seems to be dependent on an earlier source than Justin.

style of life, that they even adore Jerusalem as if it were
the house of God. (*AH* 1.26.2; PG 7A:686B-687A)

M. Williams, for instance, comments on this text as one of the reasons why we should not begin our study of the "gnostics" with Irenaeus. That is, Irenaeus included all kinds of "sects" into the umbrella category of "gnosis," "rather than a grouping defined by a list of phenomenological traits." Thus Williams would do away with the term "Gnosticism" or for that matter even the term "gnostic" as an unfit category.[13]

But related to this problem was an even greater difficulty—which Williams only hints here by mentioning Hippolytus—which has to do with the conflicting accounts given by other ancient Christian witnesses. On the one hand, Hippolytus (*Ref.* prol. 7.7-9), Pseudo-Tertullian (*Adv. omn. haer.* 3), and Theodoret (*haeret. fab. comp.* 2.3) follow Irenaeus and describe Cerinthus as a Gnostic, while Epiphanius (*Panar.* 28) describes him as a thoroughgoing Judaizer.[14] This polarized identity of Cerinthus, either as a Gnostic presented by Irenaeus, or a Judaizing Millenarian as understood by Epiphanius is also depicted by a host of modern scholars.[15] It is puzzling because a Jewish/Judaizing Christian dividing the true God from the creator of the world seems incompatible. In fact, from such apparently disparate testimonies A. F. J. Klijn and G. J. Reinink conclude that both of these notions about

---

13. Williams, *Rethinking "Gnosticism,"* 44: "In the modern construction, the 'Ebionites' and the 'Encratites' are routinely distinguished from 'gnosis.' Irenaeus, on the other hand, would have his readers think of these persons as belonging to the same general family as the other members of the catalog. Irenaeus explicitly asserts that the teaching of the 'Ebionites' is similar on some points to that of Cerinthus and Carpocrates (*Adv. haer.* 1.26.2) . . . . Hippolytus, who is dependent on Irenaeus, may be even more direct in applying the designation 'Gnostics' to the Ebionites (*Ref.* 7.35.1, 10.21.1-23.1). The point is that to the degree that Irenaeus does place all of these 'sects' in the same category of 'gnosis,' it is really merely the category of 'false teaching' rather than a grouping defined by a list of phenomenological traits."

14. Hill, "Cerinthus, Gnostic or Chiliast?" attempts to harmonize this witness with Irenaean version of Cerinthus as a Gnostic and precursor of Marcion.

15. For a list of modern scholars between 1888-1997, see Hill, "Cerinthus," 141.

The Gnostic Imagination

Cerinthus "are the inventions of early Christian authors."[16] Simone Pétrement, however, following C. Schmidt,[17] is more sympathetic with the Irenaean style of giving the account, and makes the following judgment: "Only the idea that Jesus was at first only a man like others could have linked Cerinthus to Jewish Christianity. It is also because of this idea that Irenaeus speaks of the Ebionites soon after having spoken of Cerinthus, although apart from this idea the Ebionites had nothing in common with Cerinthus as he depicts him."[18] Hill evaluates similarly: "Epiphanius has misread Irenaeus [who] had said in *AH* 1.26.2 that the Ebionites" opinions with respect to the Lord are similar to those of Cerinthus and Carporcrates. "By this he simply meant that all three [Carpocrates (*AH* 1.25.1), Cerinthus (*AH* 1.26.1), Ebionites (*AH* 1.32.1)] taught that Jesus was not born of a virgin."[19] As it turns out, Pétrement's and Hill's judgment is quite plausible, especially since the Jewish denial of the virginal birth was such a dominant doctrinal category that would have easily led some to view Cerinthus as being another Judaizer in the same way as the Ebionites.[20]

---

16. Klijn and Reinink, "Patristic Evidence for Jewish-Christian Sects," 19.

17. Schmidt, *Gespräche Jesu mit seinen Jüngern*, 404.

18. Pétrement, *A Separate God*, 304.

19. Hill, "Cerinthus," 146; for a more detailed evaluation of the sources, see esp. 143-59.

20. I would also add, however, that Irenaeus speaks explicitly of the Ebionites in other places in his *AH*. In the early chapters of book 3 Irenaeus lays down, by a traceable line of bishops, the authority of the church as the sole depository of Christ's and his Apostles' preaching in continuity with the Old Testament. He then explains that the prophets never mentioned any other God, but neither did Matthew (3.9), Mark and Luke (3.10), and John (3.11.1-6). Here in *AH* 3.11.7, just after adducing evidence from the last of the gospels, Irenaeus mentions the four gospels again, commenting on how each of the four different representative heresies was particularly tied to each of the gospels. Second, it is noteworthy that while the broader context was in reference to God, "that there is one God, the Maker of this universe"—which was the thrust of his exposition thus far—Irenaeus nevertheless specifies the Ebionite (and Cerinthian—though he does not name it as such) error in reference to Christology. This attention to Christological consideration continues in the following texts.

In *AH* 4.21.1 Irenaeus charges the Ebionites of denying the virginal birth of Isaiah 7:14 because they were following the interpretation of two Jewish proselytes, Theodotion the Ephesian and Aquila of Pontus. This he asserts at the beginning of the chapter before presenting his counter arguments for the truthfulness of Christ's taking up a human nature through virginal birth, and his famous assertion that Christ made a recapitulation of Adam in Himself. Thus the Ebionites are charged with the heresy of denying the incarnation.[21]

Thus, in surveying all of these passages where Irenaeus feels inclined to comment about the Ebionites, one central thread cannot be avoided: that they were responsible for frustrating the doctrine of the incarnation. For this reason Irenaeus identifies Cerinthus as a Gnostic, despite naming Cerinthus along with the Ebionites on account of both denying Christ's virginal birth.

THE ROLE OF CERINTHUS

As discussed earlier concerning the source behind *AH* 1.23-27, the following succinct description of Cerinthus and his doctrine very plausibly could have been available to Irenaeus from the presbyter who was once a disciple of the Apostles:

---

21. A similarly significant mention of the Ebionites is in *AH* 5.1.3, 5.2.1; PG 7B:1122C, 1123B-1124A: "Vain also are the Ebionites, who do not receive by faith into their soul the union of God and man ... and who do not choose to understand that the Holy Ghost came upon Mary, and the power of the Most High did overshadow her: wherefore also what was generated is a holy thing, and the Son of the Most High God the Father of all, who effected the incarnation of this being .... And vain likewise are those who say that God came to those things which did not belong to Him, as if covetous of another"s property (*vani autem et qui in aliena dicunt Deum venisse, velut aliena concupiscentem*); in order that He might deliver up that man who had been created by another, to that God who had neither made nor formed anything, but who also was deprived from the beginning of His own proper formation of men." This comment is in the context of explaining that the resurrection of the flesh is postulated by the incarnation (*AH* 5.1.1-5.2.3)—even a cursory reading makes it quite obvious that the incarnation of Christ is pivotal throughout this fifth book.

Cerinthus, again, a man who was educated in the wisdom of the Egyptians, taught that the world was not made by the primary God, but by a certain Power (*a virtute quadam*) far separated from him, and at a distance from that Principality who is supreme over the universe, and ignorant of him who is above all. He represented Jesus as having not been born of a virgin, but as being the son of Joseph and Mary according to the ordinary course of human generation, while he nevertheless was more righteous, prudent, and wise than other men. Moreover, after his baptism, Christ descended upon him in the form of a dove from the Supreme Ruler, and that then he proclaimed the unknown Father, and performed miracles. But at last Christ departed from Jesus, and that then Jesus suffered and rose again, while Christ remained impassible, inasmuch as he was a spiritual being (*Christum autem impassibilem perseuerasse, exsistentem spiritalem*). (*AH* 1.26.1; PG 7A:686AB)

This terse but important account serves as a rough outline of the tenets held by Cerinthus; and two particular points of his doctrine strongly indicate a discontinuity from Simon and Menander. First, unlike Simon and Menander who claimed themselves as the soteriological redeemer, Cerinthus identifies with mainstream Christianity in locating the redeemer back to Christ. In making this clear discontinuity with Simon and Menander, Cerinthus becomes a trailblazer of a new paradigm for other Gnostic teachers to follow, beginning with Saturninus. Secondly—and this is related to the first—the doctrine of resurrection is reintroduced in such a way that the Gnostic system develops and endures even to the present time.

1. *A different but old paradigm: Docetic Redeemer Christ*

In the preface to his second book of *AH*, Irenaeus gives the summation of his account of the various Gnostic doctrines laid out in the previous book.

> I mentioned the multitude of those Gnostics who are sprung from him, and noticed the points of difference between them, their several doctrines, and the order of their succession, while I set forth all those heresies which have been originated by them. I showed, moreover, that all these heretics, taking their rise from Simon, have introduced impious and irreligious doctrines into this life; and I explained the *nature of their "redemption,"* and their method of initiating those who are rendered "perfect," along with their invocations and their mysteries. (*AH* 2 pref. 1)

Two things are particularly noteworthy in this text. First, Irenaeus is a careful scholar concerned to report about the *order of their succession* all the while paying attention to detailing for his readers the many intricate differences between them. Second, Irenaeus mentions foremost the "nature of their redemption" before he lists other facets of Gnostic teachings such as "method of initiating" and "invocations and mysteries." Quite obviously, the bishop is certainly outlining his thought in a logical fashion to speak first of the "nature" of the matter. But in saying, "the nature of 'redemption'" he properly identifies the heart-of-the matter concern for all these heresies, because the promise of redemption captures the most appealing aspect above all in any proposed religion. After all, why would anyone be interested in any spiritual engagement if it does not promise enduring life in some form or another?[22] In this sense, the idea of the resurrection of a person is central to these gnostic systems, and not merely to the New Testament writers.

This does not mean, however, that we should also expect this inclusion from the earliest heresiarch Simon Magus. According to Irenaeus, Simon Magus claimed himself to have come to redeem and free from slavery "the lost sheep," and "confer salvation upon men" (*AH* 1.23.2, 3), but Simon does not need to specify this redemption theme with the idea of the resurrection. In claiming to merely appear as the human redeemer but denying himself to be truly human, he asserts to have experienced no suffering,

---

22. See Pearson, *Gnosticism and Christianity*, 201-17.

and certainly do death. Instead, he claimed to be the "loftiest of all powers" (*AH* 1.23.1), manifesting in a modalistic way as the Father, Son, or Holy Spirit, and worshiped by his mystic priests (*AH* 1.23.1, 4). Moreover, Simon was probably a miracle worker on an impressive scale, so much so that he is said to have been honored with a statue by Claudius Caesar, "on account of his magical power" (*AH* 1.23.1, 1).

Irenaeus reports that Simon's successor, Menander "too, was a perfect adept in the practice of magic," and thus he must have had enough confidence to claim that "he himself is the person who has been sent forth from the presence of the invisible beings as a savior (*salvator*), for the deliverance of men" (*AH* 1.23.1, 5). But even in this terse and only paragraph about Menander in *Against Heresies*, Irenaeus includes this detail about him: "He gives, too, as he affirms, by means of that magic which he teaches, knowledge to this effect . . . for his disciples [to] obtain the *resurrection* by being baptized into him, and can die no more, but remain in the possession of immortal youth" (*AH* 1.23.5). Still, the heresiarch claims divine origin and it is unlikely that he needs to claim resurrection for himself. But as Irenaeus as shown, this one early Gnostic named Cerinthus reintroduces the themes of Christ as redeemer and his resurrection.

Some helpful assessments have been made with respect to scholarship on Docetic Christology. On the Johannine Epistles, Raymond Brown reports that "the most widely favored identification for the adversaries of I and II John is that they were followers of Cerinthus."[23] This is consistent with the classic study by J. G. Davies who analyzed the origins of Docetism as being constitutive of four categories based on their points of departure as arising from theology (derived from the impassibility concept of the Godhead), cosmology (that matter was not capable of salvation), anthropology (that the body was evil), and Christology (that excluded incarnation and crucifixion).[24] More recently, Ronnie Goldstein

---

23. Brown, *The Epistles of John*, 65. See also Marshall, *The Epistle of John*, 17-22, esp. on 1 John 4:2 and 2 John 7.

24. Davies, "The Origins of Docetism," 13-35.

and Guy G. Stroumsa build upon the study by Davies and further express this important judgment: "The original core of Docetism did not lie in its Platonic elements, which became apparent only at later stages, but in the rejection of Jesus' passion on the cross, "stumbling block (*skandalos*) to Jews and foolishness to Gentiles," to use Paul's terms (1 Cor. 1,24). This rejection must have come first, and only then were the Docetic attitudes broadened, as it were, to include also incarnation, the idea of Christ having possessed a body of flesh."[25] This assertion that the cross of Christ continued to be the foremost and fundamental rejection in the second century is convincing also in the light of Justin's testimony in his *Dialogue with Trypho*. The intensity of the argument between Justin and his interlocutor escalates from the more "acceptable" ones (because Trypho admits that in some areas Justin has "proved his point forcibly"; *Dial.* 63.1) to the more difficult claim of the incarnation (*Dial.* 68.1), and finally to the idea of the crucified Messiah which Trypho remarks is "the most difficult to be convinced of" (*Dial.* 89.2).

This introduction of Docetic Christology among the Gnostics as belonging to Cerinthus is precisely Irenaeus' testimony. In *AH* 3.11.1 Irenaeus opens the chapter by boldly asserting why the Fourth Gospel was written: "John, the disciple of the Lord, preaches this faith, and seeks, by the proclamation of the Gospel, to remove that error which by Cerinthus had been disseminated among men." Thus the bishop also identifies Cerinthus as the *source* of the aberrant doctrine of the un-incarnate and impassible Christ. Two paragraphs later, he makes a sweeping conclusion perhaps consequent upon this "dissemination" of heresy.

> According to the opinion of no one of the heretics was the Word of God made flesh. For if any one carefully examines the systems of them all, he will find that the Word of God is brought in by all of them as not having become incarnate and impassible, as is also the Christ from above (*inueniet quoniam sine carne et impassibilis*

---

25. Goldstein and Stroumsa, "The Greek and Jewish Origins of Docetism," 425.

ab omnibus illis inducitur Dei Verbum et qui est in superioribus Christus). (*AH* 3.11.3; PG 7A.882A)

Thus Cerinthus was apparently the first to have introduced the heresy of two separate Christs, and the later Valentinian tradition continues this sharp distinction (*AH* 1.15.3). As Kirsopp Lake commented, "the amount of space given to him by Epiphanius and other later writers is not consistent with a merely local reputation," but rather points to Cerinthus' wide influence.[26]

Naturally, the next question is, if the cross was such a *skandalos* and foolishness, why did Cerinthus even bother insisting that salvation has anything to do with the person of Jesus? This becomes the inescapable question especially in the light of the discontinuity Cerinthus achieves on this matter with the teachings of Simon and Menander. By drawing attention to himself as the one who "appeared among the Jews as the Son" (*AH* 1.23.1) Simon (and Menander) basically identifies himself as the redeemer. Cerinthus, on the other hand, has no interest in promoting himself as another Christ pretender; he happily maintains that Jesus was indeed the supremely virtuous human protagonist upon whom salvation begins. This discontinuity from Simon and Menander to Cerinthus in the evolution of the Gnostic religion was probably a necessary modification for its staying power. By Origen's time, less than thirty continue to be deceived by Simon's teachings (*C. Cel* 1.57). This is hardly surprising when the teachings of Simon and Menander would still have to be sustained by their physical life and presence.

2. *A different but old paradigm: Non-bodily Resurrection*

The second doctrinal point is another necessary reformulation immediately logical for Cerinthus' "two-Christ" doctrine—namely, that the human Jesus rose bodily from the dead. Certainly, later and more sophisticated Gnostics as Valentinus and others would redefine "resurrection" similarly to what Bentley Layton describes

---

26. Lake, "The Epistola Apostolorum," 25.

it as "the intellect's escape and change of condition."²⁷ But for Cerinthus, Jesus' *bodily* resurrection in this text (*AH* 1.26.1) was clearly an insignificant detail, perhaps merely a temporal one, in the light of what Irenaeus explains further. In following up on the errors disseminated by Cerinthus, Irenaeus addresses how the Gospel of John rectifies the error of those who separate Jesus from Christ:

> The Gospel, therefore, knew no other son of man but Him who was of Mary, who also suffered; and no Christ who flew away from Jesus before the passion; but Him who was born it knew as Jesus Christ the Son of God, and that *this same suffered and rose again*, as John, the disciple of the Lord, verities, saying: "But these are written, that ye might believe that Jesus is the Christ, the Son of God, and that believing ye might have eternal life in His name." (*AH* 3.16.5; my emphasis)

Thus, for Irenaeus, Cerinthus' affirming Jesus' bodily resurrection would amount to a temporary resuscitation by the impassible Christ only to abandon the man again. In other words, a resurrection that has no salvific significance is no true resurrection proclaimed by the apostles.

This quasi-resurrection message as taught by Cerinthus seems to be corroborated by Epiphanius' account that according to Cerinthus "Jesus suffered and was raised again" (*Panarion* 28.1.7).²⁸

---

27. Layton, *The Gnostic Scriptures*, 317, here refers to the topic of the *Treatise on Resurrection*, and before A.D. 350 as its approximate date of composition.

28. Only a few paragraphs down, however, Epiphanius also gives this conflicting report: "this Cerinthus . . . ventures to maintain that Christ has suffered and been crucified but is not yet risen, though he will rise at the general resurrection" (*Panarion* 28.6.1). It is possible that Epiphanius, known for either misreading or exaggerating his sources, has simply manufactured this account here as well; however, it is not very likely that even Epiphanius would contradict himself so blatantly within a few paragraphs. Whether Epiphanius is reporting Cerinthus' actual change of mind, or more likely, different reports by Cerinthians and/or others is difficult to say. Whatever was the source of this ambivalent report by both Irenaeus and Epiphanius, it seems the genuineness of the nature of this bodily resurrection was uncertain. On the other hand, the reality of the resurrection, we have seen, was the very important qualifier for Simon Magus and Menander.

The Gnostic Imagination

From Saturninus onwards, however, a strict and absolute dualism rules so that the possibility of bodily resurrection is entirely eliminated. While Irenaeus states that Saturninus arose among Simon and Menander (*AH* 1.24.1), the point of discontinuity or a sort of *transition* concerning bodily resurrection, if not for Jesus, for the rest of humankind may have already begun with Cerinthus during his lifetime.

With Saturninus, a Docetic Christ as redeemer is maintained (*AH* 1.24.2), and the idea of adopting the human Jesus for any hope of salvaging the body is radically dropped altogether. What is added to his system is that "those who believe in [Christ] . . . possess the spark of his life" (*AH* 1.24.2). This soteriology is evidently a natural extension and a logical development from Cerinthus' Christology which asserts that only the spiritual being is impassible. Now that the bodily resurrection has been entirely ruled out, salvation according to Saturninus becomes primarily a matter of salvaging that impassible spark of Christ in man, and the destiny of an individual hinges on whether or not one possesses a "divine spark" or as later Valentinians put it, a divine "seed."

This anthropological turn, as it were, by Saturninus is decisive, since it later becomes another enduring characteristic for the Gnostic salvation myth. Thus, Birger A. Pearson properly says that salvation according to the Gnostics is essentially and uniquely dependent on the gnosis "that provides the means for the release of the soul, a divine spark in the human being that is consubstantial with the Transcendent, and its escape from cosmic and corporeal bondage."[29] Seen in this light, it appears that this anthropological inference from Cerinthian Christology turned out to be successful for propagating the Gnostic salvation myth. First, unlike what was maintained by Simon and Menander, the protagonist is no longer the object of knowledge or worship that leads to salvation: As Pheme Perkins has shown, Jesus according to the Gnostics is simply a "revealer" or an "illuminator" of the gnosis, and one with whom a mere "identification" is made.[30] Secondly, this salvific

29. Pearson, "Early Christianity and Gnosticism," 81-106.
30. Perkins, "Identification with the Savior in Coptic Texts from Nag

gnosis already resides within certain individuals who simply need to become aware of their destiny.

Notwithstanding all other variations, then, the phantom Christ acting as the *revealer* and the divine spark *revealed* within the elect became the dual emphases that persist as doctrinal traits of continuity for most of the Gnostic sects emerging after Cerinthus. In this vein, Pétrement properly identifies Saturninus as "the first almost certain example of Gnosticism properly speaking."[31] She calls him "the inventor of one of the characteristic elements of the Gnostic myth." The self-awareness of the "divine spark" as being salvific is also amply shown in various tracts of the Nag Hammadi literature.[32] But if Saturninus was clearly the first *authentic* or full-blown Gnostic, one important qualifier must be noted: Cerinthus' Docetic Christology laid the decisive foundation for a more thoroughgoing dualism of Saturninus and other innovations by the rest of the Gnostic heresiarchs.

Finally, we shall now turn to *Epistula Apostolorum*, an added testimony that it was Cerinthus who emphasized—though

---

Hammadi," 166 and 183, correctly concludes that "Gnostics did not worship Jesus," and according to the Nag Hammadi texts, "Jesus is not the object of cultic veneration," but that the Gnostics merely sought to *identify* with him. This essential role of the Jesus as revealer seems to be sufficiently attested by various NHL documents: Christ has the role of the "Revealer," "Bringer of knowledge," enlightening or awakening the believers from sleep or ignorance: *Ap. Jas.* 9.32-35; *Soph. Jes. Chr.* 93.10-12; 96.19-21; 97.19-24; 106.7-9; 107.16-108.4; 113.25-114.8; 118.3-25; *Ap. John* 23.26-31; 31.3-14; *Gos. Truth* 18.19-21; 18.11-19; 19.30-20.1; *Ep. Pet. Phil.* 133.21-134.1; *Trim. Prot.* 37.3-20; 47.22-23; 49.6-23; *Tri. Trac.* 62.33-38; 63.11-22; 65.17-25; 117.28-36; *Treat. Seth* 50.22-24; *Val. Exp.* 40.30-37; *Ap. John* 23.26-31; *Interp. Know.* 9.17-19. Pétrement, 138, asserts: "There is not, properly speaking, a search for the self. The knowledge was given without search by the revelation of the Savior. . . . Knowledge of the Savior is the necessary condition for knowledge of the self, as for knowledge of the true God."

31. Pétrement, *A Separate God*, 330-31. She sees that two lines develop from Saturninus: Valentinus via Basilides and Carpocrates and Marcion via Cerdo (Pétrement, *A Separate God*, 224).

32. Some clear examples include *Gos. Thom.* 32.20-33.5; *Gos. Phil.* 76.17-22; *Gos. Truth* 22.2-7, 13-15; *Teach. Silv.* 90.29-31; 117.3-5; *Thom. Cont.* 138.16-18; *Treat. Seth* 59.24-30; *Testim. Truth* 36.3-7, 26-28; 44.30-45.6.

erroneously—the doctrine of the resurrection for other Gnostics to follow. We shall see that while we do not have Irenaeus' account of Cerinthus' soteriology, the *Epistula* pointedly identifies Cerinthus' doctrine of resurrection to be the decisive feature of his faulty soteriology, for the possibility of the believers' bodily resurrection is nullified by the phantasmic and impassible Christ.

THE *EPISTULA APOSTOLORUM*

This 51-chapter document was in obscurity in the West before its translation at the beginning of the twentieth century, when it was first dated by C. Schmidt to be around 160-70,[33] perhaps with its Asia Minor provenance.[34] The purpose of the letter is probably edificatory or catechetical; still, as an anti-Gnostic literature there are some evidences in the *Epistula* which reveal the doctrines of its opponents, especially that of Cerinthus whose name appears along with Simon Magus in two places (chapters 1 and 7). Here are a few selected examples:

The *Epistula* begins with a general description of, and antidote against, dualism between the Supreme God and the demiurge; but already, the virginal birth mentioned is likely an attempt to confute the Cerinthus' version:

> 3 . . . In God, the Lord, the Son of God, do we believe, that he is the word become flesh: that of Mary the holy virgin he took a body, begotten of the Holy Ghost, not of the will (lust) of the flesh, but by the will of God: that he was wrapped in swaddling clothes in Bethlehem and made manifest, and grew up. . . .[35]

Only Cerinthus and Simon are mentioned again (since chapter 1). Besides giving these two names explicitly, we are told that they

33. Schmidt, *Gespräche Jesu mit seinen Jüngern*, 363. Others assign it earlier; Hill, "The *Epistula Apostolorum*," 1-53, makes a case for an earlier dating of 117-48.

34. See also Stewart-Sykes, "The Asian Context," 416–38.

35. All *Epistula* texts are taken from James, *The Apocryphal New Testament*, 485-503.

were using either the Old Testament or possibly the Apostolic teaching. In either case, Simon and/or Cerinthus are viewed as perverting both the testimony and the works of Christ, so that perhaps a different "enlightenment" could be claimed. Thus some kind of new doctrine/knowledge is assumed:[36]

> 7 Cerinthus and Simon are come to go to and fro in the world, but they are enemies of our Lord Jesus Christ, for they do pervert the word and the true thing, even (faith in) Jesus Christ.[37] Keep yourselves therefore far from them . . .
>
> 8 Therefore have we not shrunk from writing unto you concerning the testimony of Christ our Saviour, of what he did, when we followed with him, how he enlightened our understanding . . .

The *Epistula* is also conspicuously emphasizing the historical nature of the crucifixion as being applied to "the Lord," therefore the divine Christ, not just the earthly Jesus as in Cerinthus:

> 9 Concerning whom we testify that the Lord is he who was crucified by Pontius Pilate and Archelaus between the two thieves (and with them he was taken down from the tree of the cross, *Eth*.), and was buried in a place which is called the place of a skull (*Kranion*). And thither went three women, Mary, she that was kin to Martha, and Mary Magdalene (Sarrha, Martha, and Mary, *Eth*.), and took ointments to pour upon the body, weeping and mourning over that which was come to pass . . .

The highlight of the disciples' query to their Lord clearly centers upon the resurrection. More importantly, the focused concern of this text shown by Jesus' response is that there shall be resurrection

---

36. Compared to Cerinthus' doctrines Simon's are more difficult. Non-doctrinal elements may include Chapters 37 and 50: "And men shall follow after them and their riches, and be subject unto their pride, and lust for drink, and bribery, and there shall be respect of persons among them . . . they shall strive after their own advancement . . ."

37. Cf. Chapter 29: "But all they that have offended against my commandments and have taught other doctrine, (perverting) the Scripture and adding thereto, striving after their own glory . . ."

The Gnostic Imagination

of his followers, and this is elaborately explained by prophecy, its nature, and logic.

> 19 . . . Again we said unto him: In what form? in the fashion of angels, or in flesh? And he answered and said unto us: Lo, I have put on your flesh, wherein I was born and crucified, and am risen again through my Father which is in heaven, that the prophecy of David the prophet might be fulfilled, in regard of that which was declared concerning me and my death and resurrection . . . 21 For verily I say unto you: Like as my Father hath raised me from the dead, so shall ye also rise (in the flesh, *Eth.*) and be taken up into the highest heaven . . . And so will I accomplish all even I who am unbegotten and yet begotten of mankind, who am without flesh and yet have borne flesh: for to that end am I come, that (*gap in Copt.: Eth. continues*) ye might rise from the dead in your flesh, in the second birth, even a vesture that shall not decay, together with all them that hope and believe in him that sent me.

Emphasis on the prophetic fulfillment concerning the resurrection body is in reaction to Cerinthus' rejection of prophecy concerning the resurrection that ensues from the divine incarnation.[38]

Finally, in the lengthy dialogue concerning the nature of the resurrection, it is particularly noteworthy that the anthropological dualism in the eschaton is specifically drawn out:

> 22 . . . Lord, is it true that the flesh shall be judged together with the soul and the spirit, and that the one part shall rest in heaven and the other part be punished everlastingly yet living?

---

38. Cf. Chapter 31: "Like as ye have learned from the Scripture that your fathers the prophets spake of me, and in me it is indeed fulfilled. . . . Instruct him and bring to his mind that which is spoken of me in the Scripture and is fulfilled, and thereafter shall he become the salvation of the Gentiles." Also, the expression "unbegotten and yet begotten . . . without flesh and yet have borne flesh . . . for to that end am I come" seems to be a reference to the passible Christ as affirmed by Ignatius, the bishop of Antioch (*Ad Eph* 7.2).

> 24 He answered us and said: Verily I say unto you, *the resurrection of the flesh shall come to pass with the soul therein and the spirit.*[39]
> 25 . . . That which hath fallen shall rise again, and that which was lost shall be found, and that which was weak shall recover, that in these things that are so created the glory of my Father may be revealed. *As he hath done unto me, so will I do unto all that believe in me.*[40]

In sum, while Simon Magus was clearly the first *gnostikos*, that is, he "was principally the Father of all heresy—*ex quo universae haereses substiterunt,*"[41] in the broad sense as Irenaeus attests, the *Epistula* seems to focus primarily against the teachings of Cerinthus, that he two natures of Christ are *not* separated, because Christ is *not* divided. Instead, the orthodox teaching seems counteractive in detail: "As [the Father] hath done unto me, so will I do unto all that believe in me."

It seems, then, that this anti-Gnostic *Epistula* substantiates that Cerinthus had not only held a docetic Christology but also that his soteriology propounded against the bodily resurrection of his followers. Lastly, we will survey how our contemporary literatures being produced continue to reflect these dual emphases on Christ as redeemer and the concern for gnostics' resurrection—albeit non-physical.

MODERN GNOSTIC TEXTS

While we cannot survey the ever-growing gnostic literature in this twenty-first century, three famous writings are accessible on the internet. The first one, although it comes from the Valentinian Gnostic literature, "The Gospel of Truth," it is still used by the modern gnostics, as we find many such writings in the lectionary by members of the Ecclesia Gnostica:

39. Italics are mine.
40. Italics are mine.
41. Haar, *Simon Magus*, 302, shows that this is the case in the view of all ancient Christian writers.

> As we have come to manifestation in the world while we have put on the Christ and we are borne by Him until we sink down. That is our death in this life. We are drawn up to heaven as rays by the sun, with nothing to hinder us. That is the spiritual resurrection which devours the physical and fleshly resurrection.[42]

Quite obviously, Christ assumes the role of the redeemer and giver of resurrection, although it denies having anything to do with the physical. The second text is excerpted from "Gnostic Homilies" compiled by Steven Marshall:

> Easter represents a mystical experience of death and resurrection, not the celebration of an historical event. Something mysterious and miraculous happened; the disciples and early Gnostic writers experienced something...
>
> Christmas Eve, sometimes called Holy Night, celebrates the ageless story of the birth of Christ. As the divine light of Christ incarnates in a tiny babe in a lowly manger, to us this story represents the nativity of the divine light within the Gnostic soul, the coming of the royal light into the lowly frame and darkness of this world.[43]

Again, apart from the historical dimension the theme of resurrection is celebrated along with the role of Christ coming as the redemption of "divine light" or spark for the Gnostic soul. Perhaps the most important work is "The Gnostic Catechism," put together six different catecheses from France, Greece, India, and the North and South America, and includes the so-called the "Sacred Scriptures of the Gnostic Tradition" compiled together. The following questions and answers on the role of Christ and his resurrection are explicitly central to Gnostic salvation:

---

42. Hoeller, *Ecclesia Gnostica*, 136, accessed October 10, 2013, http://gnosis.org/ecclesia/Ecclesia-Gnostica-Lectionary.pdf.

43. Marshall, "Meditations: Gnostic Homilies," accessed October 10, 2013, http://www.gnosis.org/ecclesia/homilies.htm.

> Why do Gnostics then belong to the Church founded by Christ in preference to any other such vehicle?
>
> Because Christ is the latest of the supernal Messengers Whom in our age and place we recognize as our Redeemer.
>
> Why is Christ's resurrection of importance to us?
>
> Because it serves as our example for our own resurrection.[44]

CONCLUSION

Evolution for survival for the Gnostic systems included elements of both continuity and discontinuity by generally embracing two disparate impulses at the same time.[45] Irenaeus reports that these heresiarchs, on the one hand, were extreme individualists freely adapting or disregarding any material accessible to them. The fluidity of different sects with ongoing variations in all of its diversity should not naïvely rule out all human intentionality, especially when the heresiarchs were attempting to coherently communicate their secret knowledge more and more effectively. Thus Irenaeus seems justified in seeing a certain thread and pattern of continuity within the evolution of the Gnostic sects; and these loosely organized categories of shared doctrines were in line with earlier reports about them circulating and being handed down to the bishop. Hence, whether Polycarp or another unknown disciple was the true identity of the source behind Irenaeus' catalogue of the early Gnostics, it would in either case strengthen the verity of the bishop's accounts and analyses.

More important was the survival of the gnostic teachings. If the Gnostics had permanently replaced the very founder of Christianity with a personality as Simon or Menander, no relationship with Christianity would have been maintained despite the

---

44. Hoeller and Stephanus I, *The Gnostic Catechism*, accessed October 10, 2013, http://www.gnosis.org/ecclesia/catechism.htm.

45. On this idea of Gnostic resilience and survival in history I am indebted to Bock, *The Missing Gospels*.

The Gnostic Imagination

presence of many other shared metaphors, because all other issues were judged as peripheral in comparison to the person of Jesus upon whom the Great Church grounded her message of salvation. After the charismatic heresiarchs as Simon and Menander, Gnostics were adapting themselves for the greatest staying power ever since Cerinthus reinserted Jesus of Nazareth as the human protagonist of a more "refined and sophisticated" Gnostic salvation myth. An adoptionist Docetic Christology that included a quasi-resurrection message was that solution: "Christ the redeemer" and "resurrection" were two doctrinal discontinuities from Simon, but they became the enduring pillars of a paradigmatic distinctiveness for the rest of the Gnostic heresiarchs including Valentinus. This brand of Christology was much more effective for Gnostic propagation, perhaps as an alternate and plausible interpretation of some biblical texts, particularly for those with strong dualistic worldview of Platonism.

As we shall see later in the final chapter of this book, Valentinus more than any other gnostic heresiarchs made rigorous attempts to interact and draw out significance from the biblical texts. Yet, he seems to have created a worldview, whereby he sought to make sense of every data in the canonical books according to the Platonic categories. For this reason, as we had seen in our previous chapter with Judaism, the stumbling block for these Hellenistic thinkers remain the same. Essentially, they were both critical of the historical incarnation and crucifixion of a deity. The *Epistula* as an independent source seems to give such a warning against the teachings particularly of Cerinthus and even critiques his ideas of redemption by immaterial resurrection. Modern Gnostic writings give a similar testimony to these enduring themes, because after all, an enduring soteriological concern would have to be fundamentally essential for any religious movement to survive. In this light, Cerinthus may have been chiefly responsible for paving the way of survival for the Gnostic salvation myth.

THE GOSPEL AS THE CENTER
OF CHRISTIAN ORTHODOXY

1

The Creation

IRENAEUS' TEACHING ON THE creation is first of all based on his affirmation of God's transcendence and immanence.[1] The Gnostic writers' cosmogony mainly originated with Plato's philosophical "myth" of creation in the *Timaeus*, but since it lacked precise characterization, each school of Gnostic thinkers further elaborated the line of speculation by others who maintained a cosmological dualism that despised physical matter.[2] It is in this Hellenistic tradition that Irenaeus offers a Christian worldview of creation according to the Scriptures. While the Gnostic writers viewed God as the distant and uninvolved in creation other than by intermediaries, Irenaeus' understood God as positively and immediately engaging with creation because God according to Scripture is both transcendent and distinct from all creation but also freely loving and sustaining his creation. When Irenaeus anchors this argument to the rule of faith, he is appealing to the witness of Scripture as a whole over against what could be deduced from some isolated verse or text. This is because the idea of the rule of faith is not independently derived in isolation from Scripture; instead, it is a narrative of the divine economy revealed in Scripture and summarized

1. See Anatolios, *Athanasius*, esp. chapter 1.

2. Plutarch continued to write against superstition in the late first century against the spirit of credulity (see Fox, *Pagans and Christians*, 64).

in the church's books and catechesis. As such it functions like the "skeletal system" of the Scripture, as it were. Therefore, when Irenaeus says the Gnostics "say things that are like what we say, but they think something different," he means they may be citing some isolated verse on the creation narrative, but it is undergirded by an alien framework provided by an imagined cosmological dualism of the Gnostic cosmogony. Such cannot be forced into Scripture without at the same time violating its text. All interpretation must be compatible to the rule of faith and look to the objective reality signified by the Scriptures.

Secondly, to say that Irenaeus' reading of Scripture correlates with the rule of faith means that it is characterized by the narrative of redemption. Inasmuch as he understands the divine intent for humankind before the Adamic fall, but also in full view with respect to the abusive and exploitative tendencies of humans thereafter, his view of creation remains Christocentric, and only secondarily anthropocentric. This is primarily because the nature of the economy of salvation is centered upon the recapitulating work and person of the incarnate Christ, who, as the second Adam, rectifies what corruption and damage the whole creation incurred through Adamic transgression, and finally restores divine purposes to consummate fruition for all of creation along with humanity. This economy, then, finds the process of human maturation as the immediate goal, but this is necessarily measured against the original divine intent embodied by Christ who came as the human infant. Adam was not made perfect from the beginning, although he was destined for perfection.[3] In this brief essay I propose to show that, according to Irenaeus, all creation resources are to be wisely cultivated and used as instruments for the maturation of the human persons made whole in Christ as regenerate and growing into perfection. This process involves creation resources particularly in at least five areas as emphasized by the bishop: pedagogy, social order, regeneration, nourishment, and stewardship. I

---

3. Irenaeus understands the mandate "increase and multiply" in Gen 1:28 to the increasing abundance of divine bestowal on man over time. See *AH* 4.11.1–2 [SC 100:496–502].

The Creation

shall identify some key representative passages to substantiate and elucidate the implicated relationship to creation resources in the Irenaean corpus shedding light that each of these emphases distinctively applies, adapts, and thus prepares humanity to advance toward perfection.

CREATION PROVIDES THE MEANS OF SPIRITUAL PEDAGOGY OF THE HIDDEN MYSTERIES

Creation is one such pedagogical tool maturing us by helping us to appreciate the wisdom of its Author. In a delightfully instructive moment, Irenaeus explains the need for right reason to fathom the purposes and structural relationships behind the intricacies embedded in creation:

> With great wisdom and diligence, all things have clearly been made by God, fitted and prepared [for their special purposes] . . . and men ought not to connect those things with the number thirty, but to harmonize them with what actually exists, or with right reason . . . But since created things are various and numerous, they are indeed well fitted and adapted to the whole creation; yet, when viewed individually, are mutually opposite and inharmonious, just as the sound of the lyre, which consists of many and opposite notes, gives rise to one unbroken melody, through means of the interval which separates each one from the others. The lover of truth therefore ought not to be deceived by the interval between each note, nor should he imagine that one was due to one artist and author, and another to another, nor that one person fitted the treble, another the bass, and yet another the tenor strings; but he should hold that one and the same person [formed the whole], so as to prove the judgment, goodness, and skill exhibited in the whole work and [specimen of] wisdom. Those, too, who listen to the melody, ought to praise and extol the artist, to admire the tension of some notes, to attend to the softness of others, to catch the sound of others between both these extremes, and to consider the special character of others,

> so as to inquire at what each one aims, and what is the cause of their variety, never failing to apply our rule, neither giving up the [one] artist, nor casting off faith in the one God who formed all things, nor blaspheming our Creator.[4]

The beauty of rhythm and melody of this structure and interconnected order of things is grasped by right reason, which Irenaeus intimates as humble recognition of the creator, never with the presumption to rise above and beyond him. Nevertheless, Irenaeus encourages right reason and reflection to purpose "proper order of knowledge."

In the similar vein, using various objects of creation as metaphor and effective instrument of spiritual pedagogy is commonplace in the scriptures, and Irenaeus exploits them fully in reference to God's relationship to humanity. In a passage which leads up to the "symphony of salvation" Irenaeus illustrates from creation to convey a truth that unlike humanity God is never needy.

> In the beginning, therefore, did God form Adam, not as if He stood in need of man, but that He might have someone upon whom to confer His benefits ... For to follow the Savior is to be a partaker of salvation, and to follow light is to receive light. But those who are in light do not themselves illumine the light but are illumined and revealed by it: they do certainly contribute nothing to it, but, receiving the benefit, they are illumined by the light. Thus, also, service rendered to God does indeed profit God nothing, nor has God need of human obedience; but He grants to those who follow and serve Him life and incorruption and eternal glory, bestowing benefit upon those who serve Him, because they do serve Him, and on His followers, because they do follow Him; but does not receive any benefit from them: for He is rich, perfect, and in need of nothing.[5]

---

4. *AH* 2.25.1.
5. *AH* 4.14.1[SC 100:538, 540].

The Creation

When we stand in the sunlight, we benefit from receiving the rays and shine forth the light, but in no way do we add anything to the sun. Likewise, Irenaeus argues that God is never needful of us although we receive life and incorruption from him. The act of creating Adam and seeking obedience from humans, therefore, were purely determined by his goodness to bestow benefits of salvation and immortality to them.

Most significantly, Irenaeus notes that this manner of instruction, namely, taking physical objects from creation to illustrate hidden prophetic mysteries had been used by God throughout the period of the old and new covenants.

> He instructed the people, who were prone to turn to idols, instructing them by repeated appeals to persevere and to serve God, calling them to the things of primary importance *by means of those which were secondary*; that is, to things that are real, by means of those that are typical; and by things temporal, to eternal; and by the carnal to the spiritual; and by the earthly to the heavenly; as was also said to Moses, "Thou shalt make all things after the pattern of those things which thou sawest in the mount." For during forty days He was learning to keep in his memory the words of God, and the celestial patterns, and the spiritual images, and the types of things to come; as also Paul says: "For they drank of the rock which followed them: and the rock was Christ."[6]

Prophets and Apostles made use of various objects from nature or things refashioned as symbols pointing to spiritual, eternal, and prophetic truths necessary for our spiritual welfare and edification. In this vein, of paramount importance is the recapitulative significance of a tree or wood as a type. Throughout the scriptures this wood continued to speak, as it were, in Isaac taking up the wood (Gen. 22:6; *AH* 4.5.4), in Elisha's throwing a piece of wood into the water to make the axe head float (2 Ki 6:6; *AH* 5.12.3) and so forth. Finally, as much as the first Adam disobeyed "by occasion of a tree" so the second Adam obeyed "upon a tree" (*AH* 5.16.3).

---

6. *AH* 4.14.3[SC 100:546–549].

HIERARCHY AND FEAR IN CREATION IMPEDES CORROSION OF SOCIETY

Sociality and hierarchy among creatures are interdependent entities in the created order. When Adam was created, Irenaeus asserts that "both according to the inspiration [i.e., God's breath of life] and according to the formation, man was like God," according to which Adam was "free and master of himself . . . in order that he should rule over everything upon earth."[7] Moreover, this likeness to God in Adam made it possible for God to "walk and talk with the man prefiguring the future, which would come to pass, that He would dwell with him and speak with him, and would be with mankind, teaching them righteousness."[8] This means that before the transgression, Adam's likeness to God allowed him not only unhindered fellowship with God, but allowed him to optimally exercise the entrusted lordship over everything upon earth according to the measure proper to his maturity. Indeed, Irenaeus tells us that this likeness would be restored by Christ in the future so that righteousness would be taught to mankind in the context of intimate relationship with Christ. But, in the meantime, humanity has violated the divine mandate, and something had to contain the proliferation of evil in society. Irenaeus writes:

> For since man, by departing from God, reached such a pitch of fury as even to look upon his brother as his enemy, and engaged without fear in every kind of restless conduct, and murder, and avarice; God imposed upon mankind the fear of man, as they did not acknowledge the fear of God, in order that, being subjected to the authority of men, and kept under restraint by their laws, they might attain to some degree of justice, and exercise mutual forbearance through dread of the sword suspended full in their view, as the apostle says: "For he bears not the sword in vain; for he is the minister of God, the avenger for wrath upon him who does evil."[9]

7. *Epid*.11; Irenaeus, *On the Apostolic Preaching*, 47.
8. *Epid*.12; Irenaeus, *On the Apostolic Preaching*, 47.
9. *AH* 5.24.2 [SC 153:298–300].

The Creation

Pre-lapsed Adam was immature in every way, and perhaps sociality with other creatures was the most vulnerable point. For this reason it seems reasonable that God has to impose "fear of man" into his social structure as the wise and only viable means to curtail evil and violence in the face of humanity's total self-annihilation. Irenaeus remarks: "The Word of God, however, the Maker of all things, conquering him by means of human nature, and showing him to be an apostate, has on the contrary, put him under the power of man. For He says, 'Behold, I confer upon you the power of treading upon serpents and scorpions, and upon all the power of the enemy,' in order that, as he obtained dominion over man by apostasy, so again his apostasy might be deprived of power by means of man turning back again to God."[10]

The interdependence of hierarchy and sociality is manifest. The cosmos was disordered by the enemy's apostasy that involved humanity's estrangement from God, and so proper authority must be restored in order to rectify sociality between God and humanity. The grace of healing human sociality begins when Christ as man reclaims his authority over all creation by repossessing the dominion taken by the enemy and confers it to his followers.

CREATED HUMANITY PREPARES FOR REGENERATION

Irenaeus notes that the healing of the blind man in the Fourth Gospel differs from Christ's healing of other infirmities because of sin. All others caused by disobedience were healed by means of a word such as "Behold, thou art made whole, sin no more," but the man born blind received sight by an outward act, actually using the dust of the ground.

> Doing this not without a purpose, or because it so happened, but that He might show forth the hand of God, that which at the beginning had molded man . . . also the Lord spat on the ground and made clay, and smeared

---

10. *AH* 5.24.4 [SC 153:306].

> it upon the eyes, pointing out the original fashioning of man, how it was effected, and manifesting the hand of God to those who can understand by what hand man was formed out of the dust . . . in order that we might not be seeking out another hand by which man was fashioned, nor another Father; knowing that this hand of God which formed us at the beginning, and which does form us in the womb, has in the last times sought us out who were lost, winning back His own, and taking up the lost sheep upon His shoulders, and with joy restoring it to the fold of life.[11]

What is noteworthy here, asserts Irenaeus, is not only that humanity was made reminiscent of Genesis 2 that the healer's hand is really the same hand that fashioned man at first, but that this healing incident portrays the Word as the Shepherd who had redemption in mind from the beginning of creation, and that he came seeking the lost to give him eternal life by restoring his sight. For this reason, Irenaeus writes: "And inasmuch as man, with respect to that formation which, was after Adam, having fallen into transgression, needed the laver of regeneration said to him [upon whom He had conferred sight], after He had smeared his eyes with the clay, 'Go to Siloam, and wash' thus restoring to him both his perfect confirmation, and that regeneration which takes place by means of the laver. And for this reason when he was washed, he came seeing, that he might both know Him who had fashioned him, and that man might *learn* to know Him who has conferred upon him life."[12] While the restoration of the body using the clay clearly draws the parallel with the Genesis passage, there is now the need of the spiritual one, namely "regeneration which takes place by means of the laver." In this way those who are "blind" may understand that the Word the Creator intended her to progress toward maturity, preparing her to know the Word the Redeemer through spiritual regeneration.

---

11. *AH* 5.15.2 [SC 153:204-206].
12. *AH* 5.15.3 [SC 153:208-210]; emphasis mine.

The Creation

CREATION PROVIDES NOURISHMENT INTEGRAL TO HUMAN PERFECTION

God "nourishes us by means of the creation" obviously as food for our physical sustenance, growth, and energy.[13] More importantly, this was a polemic against Gnostic thinkers who had taught that creation of matter was caused by a "defect" and even resulted in chaos in the universe.[14] But Irenaeus brings forth the argument that the creator who fashioned Adam and provided food from material creation in order to sustain the body *is* the same Father we read in the Gospels providing material blessings through the Son.

> For although the Lord had the power to supply wine to those feasting, independently of any created substance, and to fill with food those who were hungry, He did not adopt this course; but, taking the loaves which the earth had produced, and giving thanks, and on the other occasion making water wine, He satisfied those who were reclining at table, and gave drink to those who had been invited to the marriage; showing that the God who made the earth, and commanded it to bring forth fruit, who established the waters, and brought forth the fountains, was He who in these last times bestowed upon mankind, by His Son, the blessing of food and the favor of drink: the Incomprehensible acting thus by means of the comprehensible, and the Invisible by the visible; since there is none beyond Him, but He exists in the bosom of the Father.[15]

---

13. *AH* 3.24.1[SC 211:476].

14. See Fredriksen, "Hysteria and the Gnostic Myths of Creation," 287–90. Irenaeus summarizes the various Gnostic interpretation of "the formation of creation [as] either in ignorance, or passion, or in defect" (*AH* 2.4.2). Furthermore, he reports that the Gnostics of various traditions follow Simon Magus who asserted that even the Maker of this world himself was the product of a defect (*AH* 2.9.2). This idea of "defect" as the source is also verified explicitly in a Nag Hammadi document: "the matter of chaos, which had been expelled like an aborted fetus . . . had resulted from [Pistis's] defect . . . [and] there appeared for the first time a ruler, out of the waters . . . 'yalda baoth'" (*Orig. World* 99.24–100.14).

15. *AH* 3.11.5[SC 211:148].

Jesus could make wine apart from the already existing substance, namely water. Likewise, he simply multiplied the loaves and the fish that were already there, although he was more than capable to create bread from "thin air" as it were, which was the case with the provision of manna. But the text purports to assert, Irenaeus argues, the oneness of the demiurge in Genesis with the Father of Jesus in the Gospels.

The second polemic against the Gnostics is the explicit affirmation of body as materiality of Irenaean anthropology.[16] Just as the likeness to God is not possible without the spirit, Irenaeus stresses that the body is indispensable to constitute the perfect human nature. In another place he says: "Now the soul and the spirit are certainly a part of the man, but certainly not the man; for the perfect man consists in the commingling and the union of the soul receiving the spirit of the Father, and the admixture of that fleshly nature which was molded after the image of God."[17]

As we had seen in the discussion of creation as pedagogical tool in the first section, the status of physical objects does not merely stop at being visible in a given time but extends toward fulfillment in the future with still more significant value. More importantly, Irenaeus' Christological interpretation would allow us to see a higher, more comprehensive purpose behind creation's role in providing food for our nurture. The physical nourishment for human material plasma points further to the Word and the Spirit as nourishment for perfect maturity. This is implicit in his response to the broader question why man was not created perfect from the beginning. Irenaeus writes: "He might easily have come to us in His immortal glory, but in that case, we could never have endured the greatness of the glory; and therefore it was that He, who was the perfect bread of the Father, offered Himself to us as milk, because we were as infants. He did this when He appeared as

---

16. Pétrement, *A Separate God*, 153, points out the subtlety of Valentinus' docetism in that "he implies in fragment 3 that the digestion of food did not take place in Jesus' body in the same way as in other men."

17. *AH* 5.6.1[SC 153:78]. Citing 1 Thess 5:23, Irenaeus views human perfection as being proper to the body, the soul, and the spirit.

a man, that we, being nourished, as it were, from the breast of His flesh, and having, by such a course of milk nourishment, become accustomed to eat and drink the Word of God, may be able also to contain in ourselves the Bread of immortality, which is the Spirit of the Father."[18] Christ accommodated himself to us in assuming the body because we were infants in need of growth before we can receive the Spirit. The Pauline metaphor on babes only fit for milk is given because our reception of the incarnate Christ is the ultimate aim. When this passage is harmonized with our earlier text on what constitutes the perfectly mature human person, Irenaeus implies that insofar as we came physically and spiritually immature in need of elementary nourishment in both realms, physical nourishment and feeding on Christ and the Spirit are both essential and necessary for human development to perfection.

STEWARDSHIP OF CREATION IS SUSTAINED BY WORSHIP

Proper stewardship ensues from a proper knowledge about authority and thereby a humble disposition proper to it. First, it must be grounded in our firm knowledge of who really rules over all creation. In the final temptation account Jesus is offered the kingdoms of this world as a return for worshipping the devil who promises that "all these things are delivered unto me, and to whomsoever I will I give them."[19] Creation, however, is not subjected to the devil's power; indeed God is the one who is sovereign over even a sparrow whether it should fall to the ground. He expounds on what attitudes of stewardship may be inferred from this:

---

18. *AH* 4.38.1 [SC 100:946-948]. Andia, *Homo Vivens*, rightly claims that the process of deification and the economy from creation are parallel; but this broad conception of human deification must also be qualified with a narrower usage in Irenaeus according to whom deification or receiving immortality occurs only after becoming "accustomed" to receiving the Spirit. See the above text and esp. *AH* 3.19.1.

19. *AH* 5.22.2 [SC 153:284].

> When placed in the exalted position of every grace that can be received, we should not, either by trusting to works of righteousness, or when adorned with super-eminent gifts of ministration, by any means be lifted up with pride, nor should we tempt God, but should feel humility in all things, and have ready to hand this saying, "Thou shall not tempt the Lord thy God." As also the apostle taught, saying, "Minding not high things, but consenting to things of low estate"; that we should neither be ensnared with riches, nor mundane glory, nor present fancy, but should know that we must "worship the Lord thy God, and serve Him alone," and give no heed to him who falsely promised things not his own, when he said, "All these will I give thee, if, falling down, thou wilt worship me."[20]

Irenaeus takes the opportunity here to insert a spiritual lesson that our desire to possess absolute power over creation would be symptomatic of having been "lifted up in pride"[21] that would eventually blind us to the devil's lie which by the way also "proceeds from him when puffed up with pride." Instead, we are given the example of Christ's humility and his teaching "worship the Lord thy God and serve Him alone." Irenaeus would not hesitate to prescribe worshipping God alone as the sure antidote against the temptation of this inordinate desire and pride to usurp God's absolute authority over creation.

CONCLUSION

Against the Gnostic theories of demiurge and his mischief with matter, Irenaeus makes unequivocally clear that God in his providence ordained creation for the sake of the human person. The design of creation as seen from various perspectives is chiefly for the human person's fully orbed development into perfection, on the ground that he is made in the image of the incarnate Son. This development is none other than the progressive unfolding of the

20. *AH* 5.22.2 [SC 153:282–284].
21. *AH* 5.22.2 [SC 153:284].

The Creation

economy of salvation that affirms the integrity of the tri-partite constitution of the human person. Therefore, the physical nourishment, the instruction for the mind, and spiritual regeneration must come into play and be sustained by a life of proper worship, all on the basis of Christ's recapitulating work. Such is the nature of salvation proper to the nature of the human person; and according to Irenaeus, the rest of creation suitably serves to bring it to perfection.

In addition, it is noteworthy that in all of these emphases, Irenaeus' prescription of how creation must be cared for does not seem to echo some of our contemporary environmentalist voices that all of nature must be kept and preserved in the pristine condition. Neither does he suggest that creation may be exploited without check or abused at will in the hands of human beings. Rather, fallen humans in need of regeneration having propensity for evil must be curbed with a healthy measure of fear, even as foreseen by divine wisdom in employing the instrumentality of social hierarchical structure.

The role of creation is to serve the development of humankind toward regeneration and perfection. This means that the second-century thinker perceives that three things occur for the original design and divine order of things to be best served. First, it entails the incarnate Person's initial healing of the individual human persons from its flawed condition to become regenerate through "the spirit of the Father." Second, all of the rest of creation may be used as pedagogic and restricting influences in preparing the human persons to this union in Christ. And lastly, those who have already begun their journey by receiving the "Bread of life" do best in committing themselves to a stewardship of developing the resources for these ends "with great wisdom and diligence" and humility as worship to God. To the extent that creation could be cared for and harnessed to nourish the *whole* person, faithful stewards cultivating with all creativity and zeal, images Christ who recycles mud to bring healing to corruption-stricken humanity, while being humbly mindful of his role though "adorned with super-eminent gifts" in service.

2

The Fall

IRENAEUS' VIEW THAT ADAM'S first sin had been precipitated by moral immaturity is well known, that inexperienced Adam had not yet reached the fullness of development.[1] But since Christ also came vulnerably as an infant who grew in wisdom and stature, one might ask, "In what specific way could Adam have overcome this immaturity as well?" Irenaeus carefully offers his explanation concerning this immaturity by comparing the two temptation accounts (Gen. 3 and Matt. 4). For him these accounts are more telling than the simple assertion that Christ recapitulated Adam's defeat. Irenaeus' thinking moves laterally between the two accounts by juxtaposing them to each other, by reflecting on the tempter's endeavors "as in the beginning," by connecting the two accounts with a significant scripture verse, and tirelessly making

---

1. Vogel, "The Haste of Sin," 443–59, is helpful for pointing out the important need of waiting, since God was not reluctant to grant incorruptibility. But his assertion that the "act of haste . . . is the root of sin" may be an overstatement; along with impatience, the fundamental nature of their immaturity emerged from their lack of proper self-concept in relationship to God. As argued in this article, Irenaeus avers that the first couple should have known the clear distinction between the created and the uncreated, that Adam should not have been "supposing that the incorruptibility which belongs to him is his own naturally, and by thus not holding the truth, should boast with empty superciliousness, as if he were naturally like to God" (*AH* 3.20.1; SC 211:386).

The Fall

additional observations covering a span of four chapters (21–24) in the fifth book of *AH*. What is Irenaeus' overall purpose for doing this? Since Christ illuminates the scriptures for Irenaeus,[2] Christ's overcoming temptation is instructive for our eschatological growth and education, that "men might learn by actual proof that he receives incorruptibility not of himself, but by the free gift of God."[3] More pointedly, the last Adam's particular manner of confronting the tempter sheds light on the nature of deficiency by which the first couple had faltered. Along this line I submit that, according to Irenaeus, Adam's self-concept was unstably disposed, that his disobedience was largely on account of a crisis in acknowledging his true identity, mainly in his relation to God.[4] In what follows, I shall present three different stages through which Adam and Eve had moved from one unstable disposition to another with respect to their true identity created in the *imago Dei*.

THE FIRST SELF-CONCEPT: *IMAGO DEI* NOURISHED BY GOD

Irenaeus makes it explicit at the outset that the temptation in the wilderness is about overturning what happened in the garden, and he does this by focusing on how each Adam had a different understanding about the ongoing intrinsic need of the human nature before God.

---

2. *AH* 4.20.2; SC 100:630.

3. *AH* 5.21.3; SC 153:278.

4. On this subject of self-understanding in relation to God, Augustine is usually recognized as the first patristic thinker. Since the knowledge of the self and of God is fundamental, he says that the human mind is wise when it not only "remembers and understands and loves itself" but is "also able to remember and understand and love him by whom it was made" (Augustine, *De Trinitate* 14.12.15). Other well-known and similar expressions on this foundational nature of this knowledge can be found in the Reformers: Luther differentiates between the law and the gospel as a twofold knowledge of oneself and of God (*Praelectio in librum Iudicum*, 1516/17); Calvin also begins his *Institutes* with an epistemology of knowing oneself through knowing God (*Inst.* 1.1.2). Irenaeus may have been the earliest on this point.

> Fasting forty days, like Moses and Elias, He afterwards hungered, first, in order that we may perceive that He was a real and stable (*verum et firmum*; *alethe kai bebaion*) man—for it belongs to a man to suffer hunger when fasting; and secondly, that His opponent might have an opportunity of attacking Him. For as at the beginning it was by means of food that [the enemy] persuaded man, although not suffering hunger, to transgress God's commandments, so in the end he did not succeed in persuading Him that was an hungered (*esurientem*; *peinonta*) to take that food which proceeded from God. For, when tempting Him, he said, "*If thou be the Son of God, command that these stones be made bread.*" But the Lord repulsed him by the commandment of the law, saying, "*It is written, Man doth not live by bread alone.*" As to those words — [of His enemy,] "*If thou be the Son of God,*" [the Lord] made no remark; but by thus acknowledging His human nature He baffled His adversary, and exhausted the force of his first attack by means of His Father's word. The corruption of man, therefore, which occurred in paradise by both [of our first parents] eating, was done away with by [the Lord's] want of food in this world.[5]

First of all, Irenaeus observes why the gospel account of the temptation also begins with the subject of eating, that "as at the beginning it was by means of food that [the enemy] persuaded man." Christ had been more than anticipating the nature of this encounter by "fasting forty days," since Christ was actually giving the devil "an opportunity of attacking Him."[6]

Secondly, Irenaeus establishes Christ's humanity against the gnostic denial of the full incarnation by pointing to Christ's words, "*Man doth not live . . .*"—an unexpected response that "baffled His adversary." In other words, the tempter's provocation to demonstrate Christ's divinity ("*If thou be the Son of God . . .*") was met instead with an answer about the Son's humanity.

---

5. *AH* 5.21.2, with a slight change to *ANF*; SC 153:266–68.
6. As Minns, *Irenaeus*, 96, comments, "it was Christ, and not Satan, who initiated this renewal of the battle in which Adam was conquered."

The Fall

But the most significant and comprehensive lesson comes when Irenaeus later gives a summary of his own comments as a way of exhortation to his readers. He says Christ "taught by His commandment that we who have been set free should, when hungry, take that food which is given by God."[7] The irony of this statement, of course, is that it seems to contradict the example of Christ. If we should take food when hungry, what was the point of Christ's refusing to yield? Irenaeus wishes to aver no intrinsic evil in eating food, but only what was "given by God" seems to be the qualifier: a limit to the provision. The truth of this double-edged sword allows Irenaeus to say that "the Lord repulsed him by the commandment of the law, saying, '*It is written, Man doth not live by bread alone.*'" And these words of Christ say something more for Irenaeus: What was it that Eve had overlooked concerning food? Unlike his gnostic opponents, he sees nothing degrading about any physical needs. In fact, hunger was not even an issue for Eve when she was tempted. Instead, Irenaeus sees that in the light of her moral and spiritual immaturity, her need at the moment more than ever was spiritual nourishment provided by God alone. Therefore this section ends this way: "The corruption of man, therefore, which occurred in paradise by both [of our first parents] eating, was done away with by [the Lord's] want of food in this world." Irenaeus discerns that while the last Adam—even in the face of his dire need for physical food—did not neglect spiritual food, the fall involved the literal eating of corporeal food by want of, and by foregoing of, spiritual food. Adam and Eve had underestimated how their nature intrinsically depends on spiritual nourishment from God, lest they become impotent and corrupt.

Does Irenaeus say anything beyond this spiritual food? Nourishment from God is obviously indispensable, but what of the means to receive it? Irenaeus would have us perceive two characteristics about Christ, that he was "a real and stable man." He was "real" because hunger dispels any Docetic idea that Christ was less than fully man; and the intense hunger belonging to a real man was kept perfectly in control because he was also "stable," especially in

---

7. *AH* 5.22.2; SC 153:282–83.

the face of enemy attack in this area of natural desire. Hence the word "stable" is no exaggeration for this man in contrast to Adam and Eve who experienced no hunger yet could not control their desires. Irenaeus does not give us an elaborate account on human desire, but his succinct overview of the condition of pre-lapsed Adam in *Epideixis* 14 sheds some light on his view:

> And Adam and Eve, for this is the name of the woman, "*were naked and were not ashamed*," since there was in them an innocent and childlike mind and they thought or understood nothing whatsoever of those things which are wickedly born in the soul through lust and shameful desires, because, at that time, they preserved their nature intact, since that which was breathed into the handiwork was the breath of life; and while the breath remains in its order and strength, it is without comprehension or understanding of what is evil.[8]

Sin has not yet entered the picture, but Irenaeus assumes that there is an important dynamic between desire and understanding. He also tells us that the health of this dynamic is influenced by the soul, which he also calls "the breath of life."[9] In the state of innocence the soul maintained its strength and orderliness, and "whatsoever" that was not good did not even enter the mind. What is unclear, however, is *how* those natural desires turned into "lust and shameful desires" which then became instrumental for "whatsoever" to be "wickedly born in the soul." Here Irenaeus is hesitant to identify this object born in the soul but seems to think that the desires (good or bad) are somehow instrumental and that the object is produced in consequence of a *process* that occurred wickedly. Of course, like Augustine, Irenaeus does not disapprove of the basic line of Plato's observation that thought, will, emotion or desires are properties of nature.[10] This means, on the one

---

8. *Epid.* 14; Irenaeus, *On the Apostolic Preaching*, 48.

9. *AH* 5.7.1; SC 153:86.

10. *Fragment* 5 (*ANF*): "The will is the mind desiring [some object], and an appetite possessed of intelligence, yearning after that thing which is desired." While desires can be misdirected or excessive, Irenaeus does not

The Fall

hand, the moral status of each of these faculties of the soul in the pre-lapsed condition was according to God's design and therefore perfectly good. On the other hand, while the faculties may each have been good in isolation, this does not preclude the possibility of disorder in functioning or coordination as a whole. In *AH* 5.9.1, Irenaeus explains how this actually occurs even when the Spirit indwells a person:

> There are three things out of which, as I have shown, the complete man is composed—flesh, soul, and Spirit. One of these does indeed preserve and fashion (*salvante et figurante*; *sozontos kai morphountos*) [the man] — this is the Spirit; while as to another it is united and formed— that is the flesh; then [comes] that which is between these two—that is the soul, which sometimes indeed, when it follows the Spirit, is raised up by it, but sometimes it sympathizes with the flesh, and falls into carnal lusts.[11]

This is not to say that Adam before the fall had possessed the Spirit of God; Irenaeus does not explicitly say one way or another. But whether Adam was actually indwelt by the Spirit,[12] or merely had "communion" with the Spirit,[13] the above text descriptive of a re-

---

condemn all desires. See e.g., *AH* 4.40.1; SC 100:974: "It is therefore one and the same God the Father who has prepared good things with Himself for those who desire (*concupiscentibus*) His fellowship . . . ."

11. *AH* 5.9.1; SC 153:106-107. The word "spirit" (used in *ANF*) should be "Spirit" in keeping with his next line: "those . . . who have not that which saves and forms (*salvat et format*) [us] into life [eternal], shall be, and shall be called, [mere] flesh and blood; for these are they who have not the Spirit of God in themselves."

12. See Andia, *Homo Vivens*, 71-72, for her comments on *AH* 5.6.1. She claims that recapitulation of the similitude was restoring the Spirit in the human person.

13. Rather than Adam "indwelt by the Spirit," "communion with the Spirit" is preferred by Briggman, *Irenaeus of Lyons and the Theology of the Holy Spirit*, 162. Along this line Cartwright, "The Image of God in Irenaeus," 175, says it succinctly that the "new humanity includes original humanity—body and soul, and improves on it—with the spirit." Even if the Spirit had not indwelt pre-lapsed Adam, the "communion" with the Spirit would sufficiently explain that Adam's maturity was not something limited to the physical and moral dimension of Adam, especially when the third Person of the Godhead

generate believer would equally apply to pre-lapsed Adam, since they both had access to the Spirit. Still, Irenaeus does not elaborate how the body, soul, and the Spirit are correlated and integrated with the three basic faculties (desire, thought, and will). He mainly states that the soul can be influenced either by the flesh or the Spirit. All natural properties function in harmony with God's design, and this orderliness proper to the person is insured when the soul looks to the Spirit for leadership. Perhaps one can harmonize this text with the previous passage from *Epideixis* 14 as follows: The soul can "remain in its order and strength" if it looks to the Spirit, because the Spirit is able to "preserve and fashion the man" by giving proper direction in keeping with the identity and vocation of the whole person. This is demonstrated by none other than the last Adam, the exemplary human being ruled by the Spirit of God: Although "*the flesh is weak. . . the spirit is willing*" (Matt. 26:41), so if a person were to "admit the ready inclination of the Spirit to be, as it were, a stimulus to the infirmity of the flesh, it inevitably follows that what is strong will prevail over the weak, so that the weakness of the flesh will be absorbed by the strength of the Spirit."[14]

Therefore, when Irenaeus is saying Christ was "real and stable" [*verum et firmum*] during this temptation in the wilderness, it certainly includes an affirmation of his full humanity. More importantly, however, it bespeaks of his steadfast character. In fact, Irenaeus has been using this expression throughout *AH* only in reference to God,[15] or the scriptures,[16] and in a surprising turn he now uses it to describe one man. But this is not completely surprising, because he has already introduced Christ in the preface of this book (*AH* 5) as "the only true and steadfast [*firmum et verum*]

---

was directly involved in giving increase (*AH* 4.38.3; SC 100:954): "The Father planning everything well and giving His commands, the Son carrying these into execution and performing the work of creating, and the Spirit nourishing and increasing [what is made]."

14. *AH* 5.9.2; SC 153:110.

15. *AH* 5.32.2(SC 153:404) and 5.36.1(SC 153:452).

16. *AH* 2.28.1, 2 (SC 294:268, 272); 2.29.2(SC 294:296); 3.11.7, 9(SC 211:160, 174); 3.15.1(SC 211:278); 5.20.1 (SC 153:254); 5.35.2; (SC 153:450).

The Fall

Teacher, the Word of God."[17] As opposed to the first couple's *infirmum*, the last Adam possessed the *firmum* by the Spirit, a disposition characterized by inner stability against the potentially unnatural movement of human desire.[18]

Essentially, then, the serpent's first question, "*Has God indeed said this, Ye shall not eat from every tree of the garden?*" was intended to let the woman set her mind of desire. Perhaps a preoccupation of mind on an immediate desire was what made her more vulnerable.[19] In view of Eve's inexperience and immaturity, her soul was unstable and gave too much or indiscriminate attention to a particular and immediate desire, thereby sympathizing with her flesh. Bodily desires may be perfectly legitimate, but if unchecked, they can sway the soul away from the Spirit, and therefore in disregard for God's spiritual provision as well. Her immediate craving for food "not given by God" had blinded her to her own identity, one whose foremost need is to be satisfied by God.[20]

THE SECOND SELF-CONCEPT: *IMAGO DEI* UNDER GOD

If humanity was made for nourishment and growth (*profectus*) both physically and spiritually through the first temptation in the gospels, Irenaeus envisions that the second temptation of Christ exposes what Adam and Eve had neglected to keep in mind, that there is a boundary concerning their estimation of themselves:

17. *AH praef.* (SC 153:14).

18. This word *firmum* (*bebaion*) for "stable" or "steadfast" seems to have been taken over by *atrepsias* in the later tradition as the stability of inner habit and power of Christ; see Maximus the Confessor, *Or. Dom.* (CCSG 23: 45.315).

19. *AH* 5.12.2; SC 153:144–45: "The Spirit is theirs alone who tread down earthly desires (*concupiscentias; epithumias*)." Here Irenaeus follows the Pauline antithesis between earthly desires and the Spirit closely. As Noormann, *Irenäus Als Paulusinterpret,* 292, observes, "the summary of what Paul calls *spiritalis* gives the impetus for him to closely examine the opposite term *carnalis*."

20. Steenberg, "Children in Paradise," 18, note 57, suggests that "intimate 'friendship with God' was absent in newly-created man."

> But he, being thus vanquished by the law, endeavored again to make an assault by himself quoting a commandment of the law. For, bringing Him to the highest pinnacle of the temple, he said to Him, "*If thou art the Son of God, cast thyself down. For it is written, That God shall give His angels charge concerning thee, and in their hands they shall bear thee up, lest perchance thou dash thy foot against a stone*"; thus concealing a falsehood under the guise of Scripture, as is done by all the heretics. For that was indeed written, [namely], "*That He hath given His angels charge concerning Him*"; but "*cast thyself down from hence*" no Scripture said in reference to Him: this kind of persuasion the devil produced from himself. The Lord therefore confuted him out of the law, when He said, "*It is written again, Thou shalt not tempt the LORD thy God*"; pointing out by the word contained in the law that which is the duty of man, that he should not tempt God; and in regard to Himself, since He appeared in human form, [declaring] that He would not tempt the LORD his God. The pride (*elatio*; *hyperphronesis*) of reason, therefore, which was in the serpent, was put to nought by the humility found in the man [Christ], and now twice was the devil conquered from Scripture, when he was detected as advising things contrary to God's commandment and was shown to be the enemy of God by [the expression of] his thoughts.[21]

In this second attack, Irenaeus sees that God's law and the pride of tempting God are interconnected. The tempter acted as if he took God's word seriously but was actually saying what was "produced from himself," namely to "cast one-self down from hence." Irenaeus reasons that the reckless jump on the basis of one's identity would issue from an arrogant heart. Similarly, Eve's decision to disregard the divine command to not eat the fruit also unveils the pride of asserting her freedom to reinterpret the prohibition, that she will take it lightly. And it amounts to an act of challenging or tempting the creator to do the same—either to reinterpret it or to go against his own word.

---

21. *AH* 5.21.2; SC 153:268–71.

The Fall

This notion of pride comes into a sharper focus in the smaller work by Irenaeus. We have seen above (*Epid.* 14) how the first couple's innocent childlike desires accompany the strength of their souls. He then immediately (*Epid.* 15) says that it was Adam's deficient[22] understanding of his own status in relation to God that ultimately brought sickness to his soul:

> But, in order that the man should not entertain thoughts of grandeur nor be exalted, as if he had no Lord, and, because of the authority given to him and the boldness (*parresia*) towards God his Creator, sin, passing beyond his own measure, and adopt an attitude of self-conceited arrogance against God, a law was given to him from God, that he might know that he had as lord the Lord of all. And He placed certain limits upon him, so that, if he should keep the commandment of God, he would remain always as he was, that is, immortal; if, however, he should not keep [it], he would become mortal, dissolving into the earth whence his frame was taken. And the commandment was this, "*You may eat freely from every tree of the Paradise, but of that tree alone, whence is knowledge of good and evil, you shall not eat; on the day that you eat of it, you shall die the death.*"[23]

Gifted with all kinds of authority over creation and having been allowed boldness to approach his creator, any rational creature might "entertain thoughts of grandeur . . . as if he had no Lord." Perhaps the soul was not paying attention to the Spirit's reminder concerning who and what Adam was in relation to God. Self-absorbed presumption did not "admit the ready inclination of the Spirit."

What, then, should have been the antidote to pride? What was the needed strategy for Adam and Eve to "feel humility in all things?" Irenaeus suggests a two-fold approach: The prohibition

---

22. Quite similar to Augustine's view in *De civitate Dei* 12.8; *NPNF*, 231, where pride is identified as "a deficient cause . . . of the soul that is inordinately enamored of its own power and despises the more just dominion of a higher authority."

23. *Epid.* 15.

is that one could not "entertain thoughts of [godlike] grandeur." The positive command is to "know that he had as lord the Lord of all." Since the idea of godlikeness was persuasive for the couple, they certainly did not remain steadfast in acknowledging their subordinate status in relation to God. In fact Irenaeus even says in one place that Adam fell by deception to "the forgetting (*obliviscendum*) of the true God."[24] Broadly speaking, then, some sort of carelessness was also involved, as "man, who, *through want of care* (*neglegenter*) no doubt, but still wickedly [on the part of another], became involved in disobedience."[25] To be sure, Eve had remembered that the fruit was forbidden, but imagining herself with the prospect and power of immortality had allowed her mind to slip into careless forgetfulness of what she really was—a creature who must remain under the lordship of the uncreated One at all times.[26]

THE THIRD SELF-CONCEPT: *IMAGO DEI* WORSHIPING GOD

The third and last temptation in the wilderness was an all-out encounter between the tempter and the last Adam. It concerned the matter of why, and to whom, worship is due. Based on the devil's false promise of immortality to Adam and Eve, Irenaeus suggests that the same issue of worship was at stake in the garden.

> He then, having been thus signally defeated, and then, as it were, concentrating his forces, drawing up in order all his available power for falsehood, in the third place "showed Him all the kingdoms of the world, and the glory

---

24. *AH* 5.24.3; SC 153:304. Forgetfulness was one of the reasons for the exhortations given by the prophets, "because by excessive negligence we might become forgetful (*multam neglegentiam in oblivionem; ameleian eis lethen*), and thus stand in need of that good counsel which the good God has given us to know by means of the prophets" (*AH* 4.37.2; SC 100:924).

25. *AH* 4.40.3; SC 100:980, my emphasis.

26. Even when human beings finally become fully mature, Irenaeus says that "being in subjection to God is continuance (*perseverantia*) in immortality" (*AH* 4.38.3; SC 100:954).

The Fall

of them," saying, as Luke relates, *"All these will I give thee,—for they are delivered to me; and to whom I will, I give them,—if thou wilt fall down and worship me."* The Lord then, exposing him in his true character, says, *"Depart, Satan; for it is written, Thou shalt worship the Lord thy God, and Him only shalt thou serve."* He both revealed him by this name and showed [at the same time] who He Himself was. For the Hebrew word "Satan" signifies an apostate. And thus, vanquishing him for the third time, He spurned him from Him finally as being conquered out of the law; and there was done away with that infringement of God's commandment which had occurred in Adam, by means of the precept of the law, which the Son of man observed, who did not transgress the commandment of God.[27]

We are told that when the situation did not seem auspicious after two failures, the devil decided to hold back nothing. Hoping to repeat the entrapment success in the garden, he resorted again to the appeals of power and glory of the world, perhaps the greatest lure for all creatures. Here Irenaeus turns to the devil's boasting words, the only Lukan phrase now inserted into this otherwise Matthean account: *"for they are delivered to me; and to whom I will, I give them* (Luke 4:6)." While the tempter's pride is exhibited here again, this time Irenaeus focuses on the falsity of the claim, since "without the will of our Father in heaven not even a sparrow falls to the ground (Matt. 10:29)."[28] Significantly, this lie (Luke 4:6) becomes the pivotal verse for Irenaeus that connects the two temptation narratives (Gen. 3 and Matt. 4): Just as his commentary on the wilderness account ends with his remark that exposes the devil's lie (Luke 4:6), his commentary on the Genesis narrative closes with on the note that the apostate "claim[ed] for himself the glory of a king among those ignorant of his apostasy and robbery."[29] In other words, this Lukan verse essentially reveals the nature of

---

27. *AH* 5.21.2; SC 153:272.
28. *AH* 5.22.2; SC 153:284.
29. *AH* 5.24.4; SC 153:304–306.

trickery in both Genesis 3 and Matthew 4 that the devil "falsely promised things not his own."[30]

These audacious claims and promise was finally matched by the equally unmitigated rebuke and counterattack by Christ. In response to the devil's brazen-faced assertion that he is worthy of worship even from Christ, Irenaeus thinks it fitting that the tempter be now exposed in his true color with the word "*Satan*," the Hebrew word that declares him guilty in judicial terms as "an apostate," that is, as the transgressor and fugitive who acted as "the strong man":

> The apostate angel of God is destroyed by its voice, being exposed in his true colors, and vanquished by the Son of man keeping the commandment of God. For as in the beginning he enticed man to transgress his Maker's law, and thereby got him into his power; yet his power consists in transgression and apostasy, and with these he bound man [to himself]; so again, on the other hand, It was necessary that through man himself he should, when conquered, be bound with the same chains with which he had bound man, in order that man, being set free, might return to his Lord, leaving to him (Satan) those bonds by which he himself had been fettered, that is, sin. For when Satan is bound, man is set free; since *"none can enter a strong man's house and spoil his goods, unless he first binds the strong man himself."* The Lord therefore exposes him as speaking contrary to the word of that God who made all things and subdues him by means of the commandment.[31]

In a nutshell, the capturing the devil served poetic justice at two levels: Since he had enticed man in the beginning to transgress God's law, it was a fair reversal that he should be conquered "through man himself." But secondly, the same instrument was used against him; while the devil used "transgression and apostasy to bound man [to himself]," Irenaeus says these "same chains" were used to bound him when he was discovered as the transgressor. The

30. *AH* 5.22.2; SC 153:284.
31. *AH* 5.21.3; SC 153:274–276.

The Fall

devil was caught red-handed, as it were, since he was caught with evidence by "speaking contrary to the word of that God." However, capturing the criminal had to be done by the perfect law-keeper in order to "subdue him by means of the commandment."

What is the logical connection between the devil's identity as the apostate and the command to worship God alone? Irenaeus takes it for granted that this duty by all creatures *was* that fundamental truth discarded by the angel. Like the Pauline history and language of sin in Romans 1, Irenaeus suggests that Adam and Eve had misdirected their object of worship from the creator to a creature: "as he did at the beginning, [namely] to deceive and lead astray the mind of man into disobeying the commandments of God, and gradually to darken the hearts of those who would endeavor to serve him, to the forgetting of the true God, but to the adoration (*adorare: proskunesai*) of himself as God."[32] Although incorruptibility was a gift furnished only by God,[33] the devil made this promise under the pretext of immortality.[34] Hence, this third and last temptation especially according to Luke 4:6 reveals that Adam and Eve had been lured away from their true object of worship to idolatry, including the *incurvatus in se* of worship—since they had neglected the most basic ontological difference.[35] For Irenaeus, the antidote to the devil's suggestion comes by declaring the counter-move against him by Christ who "spurned him from Him finally . . . by means of the precept of the law"—that is, *"Thou shalt worship the Lord thy God, and Him only shalt thou serve."*

---

32. *AH* 5.24.3; SC 153:304–305.

33. *Epid.* 7; *AH* 5.21.3; SC 153:278.

34. *AH* 3.23.1; SC 211:446.

35. As von Balthasar, *The Glory of the Lord*, 62, observed on *AH*, "all 'communion' between God and creature is based on a fundamental opposition of nature, creating and being created, which at the same time implies the opposition of being and becoming and of eternity and time." See also *AH* 4.16.4: "For the glory of God was wanting to man, which he could obtain in no other way than by serving God."

The Gospel as the Center of Christian Orthodoxy

CONCLUSION

To be sure, the devil did not tempt Eve three times as he did Christ in the wilderness, but Irenaeus infers that one can speak of three different yet related dimensions of the temptation in the garden as well. These dimensions even show different stages of temptation, as seen by the escalation of intensity in the dialogue, from implicit premise and subtlety of interrogation to explicit slander and finality of exposure. In each stage the tempter was pressing Christ to demonstrate his identity, wishing that his subject would fall into the same error as the first Adam, to do without spiritual food, to allow "thoughts of grandeur" about himself, and finally to give in to idolatry. Little did the devil know that while the first Adam thought of himself "as if he were naturally like to God," the last Adam came with the opposite mindset, for "though he was in the form of God, did not count equality with God a thing to be grasped" (Phil 2:6; ESV). Though "he might easily have come to us in his immortal glory" an infant growing into stability of disposition upheld God's program of development.[36]

For Irenaeus then, Adam's development, or the lack thereof, was clearly the issue in the garden. But immaturity is no excuse, because the prohibitive commandment had already alerted him that he is immature and vulnerable to pride and folly without this proper self-understanding in relation to his Lord. While Adam was not steadfast in this self-understanding as having been created in the *imago Dei*, the last Adam reestablishes man's identity by pursuing dependence on God's word, humility, and the worship of God. Adam did not persist in self-understanding, but Christ did and reveals that human beings live and grow into perfection only when their identity is firmly rooted in their relation to God. In fact, Christ's steadfast self-understanding of the *imago Dei* even reveals the treachery of deception against it. In this vein, Irenaeus exhorts that all believers would mature in knowledge and practice, even as we "might learn by actual proof."

---

36. *AH* 4.38.1: SC 100:946.

3

The Redemption

AGAINST THE COMMONPLACE ASSUMPTION that Augustine, if not the Reformers, "discovered" Paul's doctrine of justification by faith in the fifth century,[1] D. H. Williams paid careful attention to the beginning of the Western exegetical tradition to show that the doctrine was taught before c. 411–12, specifically in Hilary of Poitiers' *Commentary on the Gospel of Matthew*.[2] Williams' survey on both Greek and Latin works on justification, however, makes no mention of Irenaeus, a much earlier voice than Hilary as well as being an ardent student of Pauline literature.[3] In fact, Irenaeus' surviving works exceed two thousand New Testament

---

1. E.g., Stendahl, *Paul among Jews*, 85, has argued that the doctrine of justification emerged in Christian tradition when Augustine turned to Paul because of his own guilty conscience: "The Apostle Paul and the Introspective Conscience of the West."

2. Williams, "Justification by Faith," 649–67.

3. Osborn, *Irenaeus of Lyons*, 190, notes that "Irenaeus' use of Paul is not merely designed to control the damage caused by Gnostic interpreters, but rather to expound the central elements of his own theology." Dunn, *Neither Jew nor Greek*, 721, also comments: "Irenaeus engaged with Paul and theologised with and through Paul. He did not simply quote passages from Paul as though a straightforward quotation would be sufficient to demonstrate the *misunderstanding* of the 'heretics.'"

The Gospel as the Center of Christian Orthodoxy

references, a third of which are Pauline,[4] and modern scholarship on his use of Pauline epistles[5] confirm Réal Tremblay's assessment that Irenaeus was that ruthless empiricist demanding evidence and facts.[6]

Irenaeus' penchant for details aside, this study raises the question: Did "the first great exponent of Paul"[7] read the justification doctrine in a way more sympathetic with the Reformation or with the New Perspective on Paul? The numerous views that have emerged within the New Perspective on justification relating to other theological themes continue to branch out in various forms, since the justification doctrine is only one of its many features.[8] This essay will not survey these ever-growing multi-faceted inquiries on the broader doctrine of salvation, but will specifically address that deeply disputed question: According to Irenaeus, was Paul responding to a legalistic mindset in his teachings on salvific justification?

The somewhat expected difficulties of investigating this question have to do with limited sources—Irenaeus' two surviving works, *AH* and *Epid.*—as well as the availability of his comments on those controverted biblical texts on justification. Accordingly, it seems only his explanations surrounding Romans 4:13 (and similarly on 3:21) and Romans 10:3 are at our disposal for evaluation. Still, these second century comments are enormously valuable for the debate because Romans 4:13 and Romans 10:3 are interpreted in opposite directions on the particular question of whether or not legalism for justification is presupposed.[9] Therefore, I shall present here Irenaeus' interpretation of the Pauline expressions (1) "law", "works of the law", or simply "works" in Romans 3:21 and

---

4. Hill, "Irenaeus and John," 233.

5. See esp. Noormann, *Irenäus Als Paulusinterpret*.

6. Tremblay, *Münsterische Beiträge Zur Theologie*, 21.

7. Osborn, *Irenaeus*, 189.

8. A concise summary of the maelstrom of debates is given in Yinger, *The New Perspective on Paul*.

9. To my knowledge other Pauline texts on the legalism debate of justification by Irenaeus have been not found.

The Redemption

4:13, and (2) "their own righteousness" in Romans 10:3. Lastly, Irenaeus' helpful comments on the Mosaic Law are dispersed in *AH* books 3 and 4; hence, I shall offer (3) his understanding of the function of the Mosaic Law that agrees with (1) and (2).

"NOT THROUGH THE LAW BUT THROUGH FAITH"

Romans 4 has been an intensely debated text as to whether Paul was primarily reacting to Jewish national exclusivism or to the idea of meritorious ethical deeds for justification.[10] Unlike the traditional reading that the "law", "works of the law", or simply "works" refer to the entirety of the Mosaic law including ethical deeds of righteousness, the New Perspective views them as referring specifically to ethnic boundary markers, namely, circumcision, Sabbath observances, and purification laws that distinguish Jew from Gentile.[11]

Irenaeus' comments on Rom. 4 follow his remarks that by the event of the cross Christ "undid the old disobedience occasioned by the tree" in *Epid.* 34.[12] This event of undoing is then immediately identified as a fulfillment promised to Abraham in *Epid.* 35:

> Thus He also fulfilled the promise to Abraham, [by] which God promised him to make his seed "as the stars of heaven" (Gen. 15:5; 22:17), for Christ accomplished this, being born of the virgin, who was of the seed of Abraham and establishing believers in Him "as lights in the world," (Matt. 5:14) making the Gentiles righteous by means of the same faith as Abraham, "for Abraham believed in God and it was reckoned to him as righteousness" (Rom.

---

10. For a recent survey of literature, see Visscher, *Romans 4 and the New Perspective on Paul*.

11. E.g., Dunn, *The Theology of Paul*, 363, says "'works of the law' are what distinguish Jew from Gentile. To affirm justification by works of the law is to affirm that justification is for Jews only, is to require that Gentile believers take on the persona and practices of the Jewish people." See also Dunn, *The New Perspective on Paul Revised Edition*, 384–5.

12. *Epid.* 34; Irenaeus, *On the Apostolic Preaching*, 62.

> 4:3; Gen. 15:6). In the same way, we, believing in God, are made righteous, for "through faith shall the righteous live" (Hab. 2:4); so "the promise made to Abraham [came] not through the Law but through faith" (Rom. 4:13). Since Abraham was made righteous by faith, and "the Law is not laid for the righteous" (1 Tim. 1:9), likewise, we are "not made righteous by the Law, but by faith, which receives testimony from the Law and Prophets" (Rom. 3:21), and which the Word of God offers us.[13]

In this dense paragraph Irenaeus argues that Romans 4:3 simply shows that Christ's making the Gentiles righteous not by the Law, but by means of faith is a fulfillment of God's promise to multiply Abraham's seed. He then supplies two pieces of evidence to explain how this was possible: First, just as Abraham believed in God and was declared righteous, the Gentiles exercised the same faith to be declared righteous or justified (*dikaioo*). Second, this provision for righteousness was prophesied by the Old Testament in light of the purpose of the Law.

A few observations on detail are in order. First, Irenaeus says "faith," which made Abraham righteous, stands in contrast to the "law." This contrast has been (a) prophesied in Habakkuk 2:4, (b) fulfilled as promised according to Romans 4:13, (c) clearly seen by the purpose of the law in 1 Timothy 1:9, and (d) drawn by Paul earlier in Romans 3:21. Irenaeus brings this contrast between faith and law to a sharp focus when he says, "the law is not laid for the righteous." Since the rest of 1 Timothy 1:9 says that the law was laid "for those who kill their father or mother, for murderers" [NRSV]), Irenaeus is clearly not excluding ethical laws. Thus the "law" or "works of the law" to which he is alluding in Romans 4:13 and Romans 3:21 could not refer merely to Jewish identity markers. In fact, in *Epid.* 35 above, since the Gentiles are especially in view, Irenaeus is taking the word "law" in Romans 4 broadly to encompass the whole Mosaic Law, so that the ethical laws in particular will have application for both Jew and Gentile.

---

13. *Epid.* 35; Irenaeus, *On the Apostolic Preaching*, 63.

The Redemption

Second, it is surprising how Irenaeus says Gentiles are made righteous by the same faith of Abraham, when Paul did not use this language for Gentiles before in Romans. But Irenaeus is merely seeing the cause-and-effect relationship between Genesis 15:5 and Genesis 15:6 when Paul is quoting Genesis 15:6. Abraham's being justified in Genesis 15:6 (and cited in Rom. 4:3) is taken as the result of believing God's promise in Genesis 15:5, namely, to multiply his seed "as the stars of heaven." Whether or not Irenaeus is justified in reading Paul this way, he is asserting that the Gentiles are made righteous not by the law but by faith. In this vein it would make no sense to say that in reference to the "law" Irenaeus has in mind Jewish identity markers.

Now one might ask "what of the Jews who believe Christ?" For Irenaeus the Jews are not excluded if they have the same faith of Abraham. In *Epid.* 35, he is merely saying that Christ fulfilled the promise to Abraham to multiply his seed in such a great number, far greater than the number Jews alone can fill up. In fact he says a few chapters later, "He is Lord of all men, and Savior of those who believe in Him, Jews or others."[14] In *AH* we also read that Abraham's faith prefigured the pattern of following Christ for both Jew and Gentile: "[Abraham was] the father of all who follow the Word of God, and who sustain a life of pilgrimage in this world, that is, of those from among the circumcision and of those from among the uncircumcision."[15] Therefore, both Jew and Gentile will benefit by means of the same faith to be justified by God.

This takes us to our third and last observation on *Epid.* 35: Why is it that a person, or for that matter anyone, can be justified by faith? Here all discussions on justification converge inevitably on the central thrust of this text—the person Christ. It is Christ who is justifying or making righteous those who believe in God's

---

14. *Epid.* 51; Irenaeus, *On the Apostolic Preaching*, 74.

15. *AH* 4.25.1. For Irenaeus, Luke 13:15–16 shows that Abraham's faith in Christ was prefigured for the Jews: "For the Lord vindicated Abraham's posterity by loosing them from bondage and calling them to salvation . . . It is clear therefore, that He loosed and *vivified those who believe in Him as Abraham did [eos qui similiter ut Abraham credebant ei solvit et vivificavit]*": *AH* 4.8.2; SC 4:468.

promise: "Christ accomplished this, being born of the virgin," since "the Word of God offers" to anyone who would by faith "receive the testimony of the Law and the Prophets" about Christ; and it was Christ who "fulfilled the promise to Abraham." Here his two Christological assertions about justification are instructive: (a) neither Abraham nor the Gentiles are justified by the law, but by faith in Christ; and (b) this provision to be justified came through the prophetic testimony about Christ. The latter point about prophetic testimony is particularly forceful: After saying that the Gentiles were justified "by the means of the same faith as Abraham," Irenaeus uses "for" to draw a causal connection between the protasis "in the same way, we, believing in God, are made righteous," and the apodosis "through faith shall the righteous live" (Hab. 2:4) in order to draw our attention to the idea "by faith" (*ek pisteos*).[16] For Irenaeus, then, the Habakkuk text is centrally significant for Pauline theology of justification with reference to Romans 4:3, and specifically with respect to the contrast between faith and law, as he further elaborates with Romans 4:13, 1 Timothy 1:9, and Romans 3:21. The continuity of the Old Testament with the Pauline thinking reveals that "righteousness by faith" was the prefigured gift experienced by Abraham, and is now a fuller reality which Christ "offers us."

Irenaeus makes similar Christological assertions when he also has the Jews in mind on the same contrast between faith and law drawn in Romans 3:21:

> "Think not that I have come to destroy the law or the prophets. . ." (Matt. 5:17–18). For by His advent He Himself fulfilled all things and does still fulfill in the Church the new covenant *foretold by the law*, onwards to the consummation [of all things]. To this effect also Paul, His apostle, says in the Epistle to the Romans, "But now, without the law, has the righteousness of God been manifested, being witnessed by the law and the prophets (Rom. 3:21); for the just shall live by faith" (Rom. 1:17).

---

16. Watson, "By Faith (of Christ)," 147–61 also suggests that Paul adopted *ek pisteos* constructions (Rom 3.26, 30) from Hab 2:4.

The Redemption

But this fact, that the just shall live by faith, had been previously announced by the prophets (Hab. 2:4).[17]

While in *Epid.* 35 Irenaeus alluded to 1 Timothy 1:9 to explain how Abraham's faith prefigures the faith of the Gentiles, he now refers to Matthew 5:17–18 to demonstrate that Abraham's faith prefigures the faith of the Jews as well. Again, since Romans 3:21 is adduced as a commentary on Matthew 5:17–18 that Christ's advent has fulfilled the law, Irenaeus clearly does not interpret "the law" as referring to the narrower conception, that is, as Jewish identity markers, but rather to the whole Mosaic Law. Furthermore, the contrast between faith and law is drawn again when he sees Romans 3:21 and Romans 1:17 as fulfilment of Habakkuk 2:4. Irenaeus seems to take it for granted that "the law" is none other than the righteousness fulfilled by the advent of Christ, and therefore drives home the point that faith in Christ sufficiently satisfies observing the whole Mosaic Law.[18]

How does Irenaeus understand the nature of this "righteousness"? He uses another Matthean text to explain why this righteousness fulfilled by Christ is to be differentiated by another kind in Romans 10:3–4.

"THEIR OWN RIGHTEOUSNESS"

For the New Perspective on Paul, the unbelieving Jews "seeking to establish their own (*idian*) righteousness" in Romans 10:3 denotes "that which belonged to them or was peculiar to them," rather than the traditional meaning, "as achieved by them."[19] In other words, "their own" simply means "the attempt to define that righteousness in terms of the works of the law which mark out Israel's distinctiveness."[20] Thus Romans 10:3 is taken as Paul's assertion of

---

17. *AH* 4.34.2; SC 100: 848, 850; emphasis mine.

18. See also *AH* 4.34.2.

19. Dunn, *The New Perspective*, 11, 373, and 388 n. 24. He credits the exegetical insight of *idios* to Howard, "Christ the End of the Law," 331–7.

20. Dunn, *Romans 9–16*, 588.

antithesis between "'the righteousness of God' as a protest against Jewish restrictiveness."[21]

For Irenaeus, Christ's rebuking of the Pharisees in Matthew 15 and 23 demonstrates what Paul has in mind concerning the nature of "their own righteousness" in Romans 10:3. He says Christ exposes the Pharisaical traditions that opposed the Mosaic Law in Matthew 15, a comprehensive and representative account of the kind of righteousness Judaism taught and exemplified during the Second Temple Period:

> "They bind heavy burdens, and lay them upon men's shoulders; but they themselves will not so much as move them with a finger" (Matt. 23:4). . . [Christ] did throw blame upon those persons, because they repeated indeed the words of the law, yet were *without love*. And for this reason were they held as being unrighteous as respects God, and as respects their neighbors. As also Isaiah says: "This people honoreth Me with their lips, but their heart is far from Me: howbeit in vain do they worship Me, teaching the doctrines and the commandments of men." (Matt. 15:8–9). He does not call the law given by Moses commandments of men, but the traditions of the elders themselves which they had invented, and in upholding which they made the law of God of none effect, and were on this account also not subject to His Word. For this is what Paul says concerning these men: "For they, being ignorant of God's righteousness, and going about to establish their own righteousness, have not submitted themselves to the righteousness of God. For Christ is the end of the law for righteousness to everyone that believeth" (Rom. 10:3–4).[22]

In this lengthy text, Irenaeus carefully paints for us the righteousness of the wrong kind. As he begins this section in the previous

---

21. Dunn, *The New Perspective*, 373. Noting that Paul's teaching was formulated in a polemical manner, Dunn raises the question, "what was Paul reacting against?" and answers "Jewish restrictiveness." Similarly, Wright, "The Letter to the Romans," 655, says it refers to the Jews setting up a status of covenant membership, "a status for all Jews, and only for Jews."

22. *AH* 4.12.4; SC 100: 516.

The Redemption

paragraphs, Irenaeus also mentions that these Pharisees (a) either "pretended to observe from the law" or (b) "set up a spurious law" which was "contrary to the [true] law,"[23] thereby nullifying and mutilating the Decalogue, the fifth commandment in particular.[24] Irenaeus adds in the above text that even when they "repeated the words of the law," they were "without love." Consequently, Christ cast blame on them "as being unrighteous as respects God, and as respects their neighbors." In the final analysis, because the Decalogue was twisted and replaced by the commandments of men, the law of God was opposed by their own righteousness; as such, it is an illustration of Paul's assessment of Judaism: "being ignorant of God's righteousness, [they were] going about to establish their own righteousness" (Rom. 10:3).[25]

But from where does this broken righteousness come? Irenaeus actually furnishes us with the real cause of these "inventions" and mutilations of the Decalogue as being rooted in a particular strand of disease: a preoccupation with human achievement and zeal performed in order to be seen by men. He identifies this root at the outset introducing the section cited above:

> To scoffers, and to those not subject to God, but who follow outward purifications for the praise of men and to those who pretend that they do themselves observe *more than what has been prescribed*, as if preferring their own zeal to God Himself while within they are full of hypocrisy, and covetousness, and all wickedness.[26]

---

23. *AH* 4.12.1.

24. Matt 15:3 is in reference to violation of the fifth commandment in Matt 15:4–6. Noormann assumes that Irenaeus has rabbinic Halacha in view: *Irenäus Als Paulusinterpret*, 402 n. 152.

25. Bacq, *De L'ancienne À La Nouvelle Alliance Selon S. Irénée*, 107, comments on this section: "in reality they were hypocritically attached to their own 'tradition' which was contrary to the Law... Isaiah already reproached them with 'mixing wine with water' (Isa 1:22), that is to say, adding purely human traditions to the 'precept of God.' Wanting to defend these traditions, 'they did not submit to the Law of God' (Rom 10:3) which 'directed them to Christ' and prepared them to receive it, as Paul asserts (cf. Gal 3:24)."

26. *AH* 4.11.4; SC 100:508; emphasis mine.

The Gospel as the Center of Christian Orthodoxy

To be sure, people's pretentious attitude to the law was not uniform, but was varied by a range of different positions even among religious leaders. But to whatever extent they were motivated by the praise of men, Irenaeus thinks that observing "more than what has been prescribed" also implies "preferring their own zeal to God himself." Moreover, this idea of zeal or self-achievement apart from God was also a blind pursuit, because Irenaeus intimates that beyond their pretensions to deceive others, self-deception was also at play.[27] This sort of blindness would indicate that they sincerely thought of themselves as scrupulous keepers of the law. For Irenaeus then, Paul was not referring to Jewish ethnic pride over against the Gentiles in Romans 10:3. Instead, he was speaking more against religious leaders at different levels who had a prideful estimate about themselves above their own kin, namely other Jews: They claimed to "observe more than what has been prescribed," when in reality they were inventing alterations on the Law of Moses including the fifth commandment. These false notions about themselves helped them to pretentiously boast about their piety, trumpeting that they were unlike the tax collectors and sinners.

If Irenaeus understood that these pretensions and overzealous observances of the Mosaic Law constituted the righteousness of "their own," how does he define the nature of the true righteousness of God? For this he cites Romans 10:4 ("Christ is the end of the law for righteousness to everyone that believes") as an assertion that Christ offers himself as the true righteousness to be received by faith, revealed to Moses and fully manifested as Savior in his actual coming to be received in faith.[28] This brings us to the question of how Irenaeus understood the exact function of the Mosaic Law in preparation for his coming.

---

27. Irenaeus speaks of God's "compassion to their blindness": *AH* 4.17.2 and 4.18.3.

28. The text ends thus: "And how is Christ the end of the law . . . it [is] customary from the beginning with the Word of God to ascend and descend for the purpose of saving those who were in affliction": *AH* 4.12.4.

The Redemption

THE FUNCTIONS OF THE MOSAIC LAW

In Books 3 and 4 of *AH*, Irenaeus seems to hold a similar view with Justin Martyr concerning the three major functions of the law to prepare the way for the incarnation.[29] The law was set up to *condemn* all violations, somehow advance or *mature* people to move from servitude to freedom, and lastly, help them *anticipate* salvation in the coming Christ.

First, the law as a pedagogue needed to condemn all trespasses as a constant reminder of the presence of sin in human beings. He says the law placed "a weighty burden upon man, who had sin in himself, showing that he was liable to death . . . [and] the law merely made sin to stand out in relief, but did not destroy it."[30] The law's constant reminder plus the inability of the knowledge of the law to destroy sin added up to condemnation. Irenaeus concludes that this condemning function was temporary until the time of Christ's resurrection in the New Covenant: "The Head rose from the dead, so also the remaining part of the body—of every man who is found in life—when the time is fulfilled of that *condemnation* (*impleto tempore condemnationis*) which existed by reason of disobedience."[31]

The second function of the law as a pedagogue was about *maturing* the Jews and encouraging them to "run to Christ." In *AH* 4.16.2–4, Irenaeus uses Deuteronomy 5–8 as the proof text to explain why God drafted the Mosaic Covenant with the Jews after the Exodus and not with the patriarchs before them. Previously, the forefathers needed no elaborate system of statutes beyond the basic commands to love God and to be kind to one's neighbor. Enoch, Noah, and Abraham were far from perfect, yet they

---

29. The accounts by Justin and Irenaeus differ on detail, but they both hold to the similar tripartite functions (ethics, historical dispensation, and prophecy) of the Mosaic Law. See the excellent analysis and presentation by Stylianopoulos, *Justin Martyr and the Mosaic Law*, esp. chapter 2.

30. *AH* 3.18.7.

31. *AH* 3.19.3; SC 211:382.

had "loved the God who made them and did no injury to their neighbor."³² Unfortunately, while the Jews were living in Egypt,

> this righteousness and love to God had passed into oblivion, and became extinct in Egypt, [and] God led the people with power out of Egypt, in order that man might again become the disciple and follower of God . . . who prepares man for His friendship through the medium of the Decalogue.³³

Hence God's giving of the Decalogue was timely and pedagogical, but the severity of their hardened hearts revealed that the giving of the Decalogue—though otherwise appropriate for human nature—was not enough to educate the Jews to be devoted to God.³⁴ In this poignant passage Irenaeus relates, therefore, how God accommodated to their immaturity by adding cultic precepts which later became even more slavish measures beyond the Decalogue:

> [As Moses says] "He wrote them on two tables of stone, and gave them to me". . . . But when they turned themselves to make a calf, and had gone back in their minds to Egypt, desiring to be slaves instead of free-men, *they were placed for the future in a state of servitude suited to their wish*—a slavery which did not indeed cut them off from God, but subjected them to the yoke of bondage.³⁵

The Decalogue was already a remedial measure to bring back the Jews into friendship with God, yet another step was inevitable for these wayward Jews. In view of their unruliness, giving of extra statutes actually started out as merciful divine accommodations and encouragements for them to stay within the bounds, applying the ethics of the Decalogue graciously on various domestic and civic matters. One such example permitted the issuing of divorce

---

32. *AH* 4.16.3.

33. *AH* 4.16.3; emphasis mine.

34. *AH* 4.15.1: "For God at the first, indeed, warning them by means of natural precepts, which from the beginning He had implanted in mankind, that is, by means of the Decalogue."

35. *AH* 4.15.1; emphasis mine.

The Redemption

certificates.[36] Obviously, the demands of the seventh commandment became more lenient, and this "lowering of the bar" to spare them from immediate punishment was an expression of divine mercy inviting them to repentance. But when the Jews took divine kindness for granted with rude and primitive response, thus further hardening their hearts, the result was deeper enslavement to sin. Meanwhile, Irenaeus says, "God permitted similar indulgences for the benefit of His people . . . [that] being restrained by Him, should not revert to idolatry, nor apostatize from God, but learn to love Him with the whole heart."[37]

Among many of these adjustments for temporary fixes insofar as they were discouraging complete apostasy, some were cultic laws multiplied to the people by Moses.[38] Whenever a commandment was violated, the requirements of a particular sacrificial law would spell out their sins, so that their guilt would be confronted, repented of, and forgiven, thereby teaching them to engage their heart in contrition, repentance, and thanksgiving. Such was the gracious divine intent behind cultic precepts to make accommodation and restoration for ethical, civic, and ceremonial violations in the light of their weakness and immaturity. But contrary to God's desire to cultivate this religion of the heart, they separated themselves from Yahweh by resorting to mere external performances, simply to avoid his wrath, simply as a means to pay their dues, as it were.[39] While some Jews abstained from the love of God and persisted in their externalized religion, others began to learn and mature from listening to the prophets like Samuel and David, as Irenaeus says: "Still clearer, too, does he speak of these things in the fiftieth Psalm: 'For if Thou hadst desired sacrifice, then would

---

36. *AH* 4.15.2.
37. *AH* 4.15.2; emphasis mine.
38. *AH* 4.16.5.
39. *AH* 4.17.1: "He perceived them neglecting righteousness, and abstaining from the love of God, and imagining that God was to be propitiated by sacrifices and the other typical observances."

I have given it: Thou wilt not delight in burnt-offerings. The sacrifice of God is a broken spirit.'"[40]

The third and last function of the law was somewhat prophetic. It was exhorting the Jews to look forward to the promise of the ultimate salvation by faith in Christ:

> For the law never hindered them from believing in the Son of God; nay, but it even exhorted them so to do, saying that men can be saved in no other way from the old wound of the serpent than by believing in Him who, in the likeness of sinful flesh, is lifted up from the earth upon the tree of martyrdom.[41]

On the one hand, the law pointed to Christ in light of the continuity between the Decalogue and Christ's commands, for in reference to the Sermon on the Mount Irenaeus says that Christ's extending and fulfilling the laws is shown from his words. On the other hand, Irenaeus asserts that Christians who believe like Abraham no longer needed the law in the new legislation. He says Christ is all we need because trusting him enables us to love God and our neighbor, which sums up the law.[42]

For Irenaeus then, God never desired his relationship with the people in the Old Testament to become legalistic. This is partly discernible, says Irenaeus, from the faithful patriarchs who had maintained this love for God and neighbor. But when the period of slavery in Egypt had induced the Jews to neglect their devotion to God, legalism emerged from many of them who turned what was once a heart relationship with God to a mere servitude by disengaging the heart. Of course, the law did not convict and train the heart of every Jewish person,[43] but some who had been prepared

---

40. *AH* 4.17.1.

41. *AH* 4.2.7.

42. *Epid.* 95–96; Irenaeus, *On the Apostolic Preaching*, 97–98: "we should no longer turn back . . . to the former legislation, for we received the Lord of the Law, the Son of God, and through faith in Him we learn to love God with [our] whole heart and our neighbour as ourselves . . . . Therefore we do not need the Law as a pedagogue."

43. This variation would also explain what Dunn, "Paul, Grace and *ERGA*

The Redemption

by the law were indeed driven to run to Christ to find salvation. He says, "But as many as feared God, and were anxious about His law (*timebant Deum et solliciti erant circa legem ejus*), these *ran to Christ,* and were all saved."[44] Irenaeus, then, seems to closely follow Paul and Justin Martyr that the Mosaic Law was a pedagogue until the New Covenant. Specifically, law's condemning, and then maturing roles were intended for that heart-relationship with Yahweh, so that they would be prepared to have faith in Christ. While few remnants were properly prepared, many unfortunately were satisfied to keep an externalized religion which then expressed itself as a form of legalism.

CONCLUSION

On the significance of the Decalogue James Dunn says: "Israel did not gain God's acceptance by virtue of their law-keeping. The law was given not to show Israel how to win Yahweh's favor. It was given to show the already favored people how to live as Yahweh's people."[45] Here, Irenaeus would agree insofar as those faithful remnants are concerned; however, he would also point out that not all Israel were spiritual Israel.[46] The proponents of the New Perspective on Paul seem to view that most of the Jews of the Second Temple period had a decent understanding of this Mosaic Law except for nationalistic pride. But for Irenaeus the Jews' failure to understand God's true intent in giving the law and the covenant had to do primarily with neglecting their inner struggle to love God. It was the need of coming to grips with one's existential interiority, to put one's honest relationship with God above how one

---

NOMOU," 269, recognizes: "Second Temple and rabbinic writings may well be less consistent than Sanders argued." See Gathercole, *Where is Boasting?*, esp. 37–111.

44. *AH* 4.2.6–7; SC 100:410; emphasis mine.

45. Dunn, "Paul, Grace and *ERGA NOMOU*," 269.

46. *AH* 4.15.1: Many were led to idolatry, for they "offered to [God] sacrifices and oblations for forty years in the wilderness and took up the tabernacle of Moloch, and the star of the God Remphan."

had or had not performed outwardly. Irenaeus' reading of Paul's reaction to "their own righteousness" during the Second Temple period had to do with them congratulating themselves in taking the reductionist interpretation of the law whereby they lacked inner righteousness and love for God, apparently characteristic of the unruly Israel rebuked by the prophets as well. For Irenaeus, their desire "to be seen by others," prizing and preferring their own zeal to God himself, and the mere focus on the external observance of the law made it easier for them to give way to legalism and pretensions.

4

The Consummation

IT IS BY MEANS of trinitarian theology that Irenaeus connects the end with the beginning, as Colin Gunton observed in his book, *The Triune Creator*: "it is perhaps the notion of creation as that which is directed to an eschatological perfection which is one of the most neglected features of Irenaeus' thought."[1] Since then, Irenaean studies in relation to the trinity have begun to appear in recent years, yet no substantial attention has yet been given to a trinitarian analysis on the doctrine of the resurrection.[2] To fill this gap the main purpose of this article is to consider how Irenaeus defends the resurrection doctrine by means of his trinitarian hermeneutic. I will frame this essay by introducing a text which

---

1. Gunton, *The Triune Creator*; notably, he has written a trinitarian reading of the doctrine of creation, Christology, atonement, baptism and the Church before his untimely death 2003.

2. As Barnes, "Irenaeus' Trinitarian Theology," 67–107, has noted, "It is strange to observe that the most substantial account of Irenaeus" Trinitarian theology remains that of Lebreton in his 1928 *Histoire du Dogme de la Trinité*. Since then, Lashier has published his dissertation, *Irenaeus on the Trinity*, but the resurrection doctrine is wholly unaddressed. While Briggman's *Irenaeus of Lyons and the Theology of the Holy Spirit* makes helpful scattered comments with respect to the Holy Spirit, it does not provide a trinitarian analysis or reading of the resurrection doctrine.

roughly functions as a "prologue" to the twenty-four chapters[3] on the resurrection in the final book of *AH*. An analysis of these chapters indicates that this prologue succinctly introduces what he expands and elaborates more fully in the rest of the text. Irenaeus is typically deliberate at every turn, and this prologue helpfully orients us with a big picture, even as he situates his argument within the whole divine economy:

> We—who were but lately created by the only best and good Being, by Him also who has the gift of immortality, having been formed after His likeness (predestinated, according to the prescience of the Father, that we, who had as yet no existence, might come into being), and made the first-fruits of creation—have received, in the times known beforehand [the blessings of salvation], according to the ministration of the Word, who is perfect in all things, as the mighty Word, and very man, who, redeeming us by His own blood in a manner consonant to reason, gave Himself as a redemption for those who had been led into captivity. And since the apostasy tyrannized over us unjustly, and, though we were by nature the property of *the omnipotent God*, alienated us contrary to nature, rendering us its own disciples, the Word of God, powerful in all things, and not defective with regard to His own justice, did righteously turn against that apostasy... Since the Lord thus has redeemed us through His own blood, giving His soul for our souls (*psychen autou anti tes hemeteras psyches*), and His flesh for our flesh, and has also poured out the Spirit of the Father for the union and communion (*henosin kai koinonian*) of God and man, imparting indeed God to men *by means of the Spirit*, and, on the other hand, attaching man to God *by His own incarnation*, and bestowing upon us at His coming immortality durably and truly, by means of communion with God—all the doctrines of the heretics fall to ruin.[4]

---

3. I find these chapter divisions by Donovan, *One Right Reading* satisfying; chapters 1–24 deal with Irenaeus' arguments for the resurrection, and chapters 25–36 have to do with the Millennial Kingdom.

4. *AH* 5.1.1–2 (SC 153.16–21); emphasis mine.

The Consummation

This prologue lays out at least three main features, all of which are inter-related to one another and embedded in the chapters that follow. These features serve as clues in finding some sort of order and unity to an otherwise lengthy discourse laden with a dense labyrinth of diverse exegetical claims. The first and the most obvious is the bishop's use of an overarching salvation narrative, functioning like a *regula fidei*, which is typical of Irenaeus for dealing with controversies. The second feature is the naming of all three divine persons signifying the overall structural design of these chapters that follow. The direct involvement of the three is made explicit in the introductory chapters (*AH* 5.1–5.2), followed by a discussion of the roles of the Father (*AH* 5.3–5.5), the Spirit (*AH* 5.6–5.13), and the Son (*AH* 5.14–5.24). Lastly, the prologue emphasizes agency of the Son, for he applies this redemption first by "imparting God to men by means of the Spirit," and then by "attaching man to God."

But how exactly do these features draw out a persuasive argument for the resurrection? In what follows, I should like to identify three activities that make the resurrection possible, which Irenaeus describes as belonging to the three divine persons respectively. Since the end is connected with the beginning for Irenaeus, I propose that these divine activities for the resurrection are similar to their activities in the making of Adam. Naturally, I shall demonstrate that these descriptions for the creation of Adam found elsewhere in the Irenaean corpus is repeated and amplified for the Christian resurrection in these chapters in the fifth book of *AH*. But first, I shall present how Irenaeus sets out his whole defense for "the salvation of the flesh" by connecting the end with the beginning.

THE END IS CONNECTED TO THE BEGINNING

Irenaeus follows the Pauline thesis that the bodily resurrection is rooted in Christ's resurrection, and he also notes that his opponents view against the salvation of the flesh stems from their rejection of Christ's incarnation. But he further points out that this rejection of the incarnation is caused by a failure to see the whole economy of salvation and consider why and how God had created Adam in the first place:

> For He would not have been one truly possessing flesh and blood, by which He redeemed us, unless He had summed up in Himself the ancient formation of Adam. Vain therefore are the disciples of Valentinus who put forth this opinion, in order that they may *exclude the flesh from salvation* and *cast aside what God has fashioned*. Vain also are the Ebionites, who do not receive by faith into their soul the union of God and man but who remain in the old leaven of [the natural] birth, and who do not choose to understand that the Holy Ghost came upon Mary, and the power of the Most High did overshadow her (Luke 1.35) . . . Therefore do these men reject the commixture of the heavenly wine, and wish it to be water of the world only, not receiving God so as to have union with Him, but they remain in that Adam who had been conquered and was expelled from Paradise: *not considering that as, at the beginning* of our formation in Adam, that breath of life which proceeded from God, having been *united* to what had been fashioned, animated the man, and manifested him as a being endowed with reason; *so also, in [the times of] the end* (sic in fine), the Word of the Father and the Spirit of God, having become *united* with the ancient substance of Adam's formation, rendered man living and perfect, receptive of the perfect Father, in order that as in the natural [Adam] we all were dead, so in the spiritual we may all be made alive. *For never at any time did Adam escape the hands of God*, to whom the Father speaking, said, "Let Us make man in Our image, after Our likeness." And for this reason, in the last times (*fine*), not by the will of the flesh, nor by the will of man, but by the good pleasure of the Father (John 1.13), His hands formed a living man, in order that Adam might be created [again] after the image and likeness of God.[5]

---

5. *AH* 5.1.2–3 (SC 153.24–29); emphasis mine.

The Consummation

First, delineating Irenaeus' line of reasoning in this rather dense polemical text is in order. Both Valentinians and the Ebionites reject "the union of God and man," says Irenaeus, because they have an aversion against uniting anything spiritual with the material.[6] He then seems to criticize both groups on their own turf, as it were, finding some common ground, as he knew they both were interpreting the Genesis account of the creation of Adam. To be sure, the Valentinians interpreted that the "fluid matter" rather than the earth was used as part of the material formation of Adam; but they, too, nevertheless affirmed that the Demiurge "breathed into [Adam]" that "substance . . . called the spirit of life" (*AH* 1.5.5). Irenaeus' appeal, of course, is the goodness of God who did not abandon natural Adam to remain dead, but that this breathing into the first Adam was proleptic of still another union between the material and the spiritual; for "*as, at the beginning of our formation in Adam . . . so also, in [the times of] the end* the Word of the Father and the Spirit of God, having become united with the ancient substance of Adam's formation rendered man living and perfect." Irenaeus concludes with the Johannine text that restoring the image and likeness of God by granting resurrection to Adam was God's intention from the beginning, for "never at any time did Adam escape the hands of God."

THE FATHER WHO CREATED ADAM GRANTS ADOPTION

In keeping with the trinitarian structure of his defense, Irenaeus begins by focusing on the Father's wisdom and power (*AH* 5.3–5). He addresses objections like why physical death was permitted in the first place by pointing to God's wisdom for instilling in us

---

6. This is certainly from Plato as Hippolytus explicitly says: "Such, to run through the chief points, is the established doctrine of Pythagoras and Plato. It is from this doctrine—not from the Gospels—that Valentinus pieced together his own heresy": *toiaute tis, os en kephalaiois eipein epelthonta, he puthagorou kai platonos sunesteke doxa, aph' hes oualentinos, ouk apo ton euanggelion* (Hippolytus, *Refutation of All Heresises*, 406–407).

humility and dependence on the Creator. Moreover, Irenaeus reiterates: to see "that He is powerful in all these respects, we ought to perceive from our origin, inasmuch as God, taking dust from the earth, formed man. . . . [Then, we will conclude that] the Lord has power to infuse life into what He has fashioned, and since the flesh is capable of being quickened" (*AH* 5.3.3). Enoch and Elijah are such examples of this capacity inherent in the flesh, for they were "translated in the same body . . . thus pointing out by anticipation the translation of the just" (*AH* 5.5.1).

But how does Irenaeus connect the end with the beginning with respect to the activity of the Father? As James Wiegel has convincingly shown the trinitarian structure of the *Epideixis*,[7] chapter 8 opens the discourse specifically on the Father's activity as Creator:

> And the Father is called by the Spirit "Most High" and "Almighty" and "Lord of Host" that we may learn [that] the God, this one Himself, He is the Maker of heaven and earth and the whole world, the Creator of angels and men, and the Lord of all, by whom all things exist, and from whom all things are nourished—merciful, compassionate, good, righteous, the God of all—both of the Jews and of the Gentiles and of the faithful: However, to the faithful He is as Father, since "in the last times" He opened the testament of the *adoption (adoptionis; huiothesia)* as sons.[8]

The Father is first recognized as the Creator of angels and men, but after the work of creation his activity is identified further as granting adoption to the faithful. This two-sequence acts of the Father are lucidly translated by J. Robinson: "To them that believe He is

---

7. Wiegel, "The Trinitarian Structure of Irenaeus' *Demonstration*" 113–39. He proposes the structural divisions as follows: the importance of right thought and right action (*Epid.* 1–3); Trinitarian baptismal seal (*Epid.* 3–7); discourse on God as Creator (*Epid.* 8–30); salvific advent of the Son (*Epid.* 31–42a); and prophetic activity of the Holy Spirit (*Epid.* 42b–97). Perhaps this article invite studies to explore trinitarian readings of other doctrines by Irenaeus.

8. *Epid.* 8; (SC 406:94).

The Consummation

as Father, for in the end of the times He opened up the covenant of adoption."[9] This means that Irenaeus distinguishes those who will be adopted from those who were merely created, as he makes this distinction explicit to the Ebionites earlier in book three of *AH*:

> Those who assert that He was simply a mere man, begotten by Joseph, remaining in the bondage of the old disobedience are in a state of death having been not as yet joined to the Word . . . The Word says, mentioning His own gift of grace: "I said, Ye are all the *sons of the Highest* (*filii Altissimi omnes*), and gods; but ye shall die like men". He speaks undoubtedly these words to those who have not received the gift of *adoption* (*adoptionis*), but who despise the incarnation of the pure generation of the Word of God, defraud human nature of promotion into God, and prove themselves ungrateful to the Word of God, who became flesh for them.[10]

Irenaeus apparently assigns two different meanings to sonship in this passage. The Ebionites are included when the Word calls them "sons of the Highest," yet they are also identified as "those who have not received the gift of adoption" because they reject the incarnation. Clearly, then, Irenaeus employs sonship as continuity of expression between the Father's activity of creation with that of the final adoptive sonship of the faithful. But the discontinuity is also emphasized by the bishop in his defense of the resurrection, even as he distinguishes the efficacy of divine Spirit from that of the created breath of God:

> Thus does he attribute the Spirit as peculiar to God which in the last times He pours forth upon the human race by the *adoption of sons* (*adoptionem filiorum*); but [he shows] that breath was common throughout the creation and points it out as something created. Now what

---

9. Robinson's translation in Mackenzie, *Irenaeus' Demonstrations*, 3.
10. *AH* 3.19.1; (SC 211:372); emphasis mine.

has been made is a different thing from him who makes it. The breath, then, is temporal, but the Spirit eternal.[11]

Notwithstanding discontinuity between the breath and the Spirit, the manner in which the Father acts to grant adoption remains the same to his act in making man. In his aim to perfect the image and likeness in the faithful, God does so with his hands, the Son and the Spirit:

> The Father bears the creation and His own Word simultaneously, and the Word borne by the Father grants the Spirit to all as the Father wills. To some He gives after the manner of creation what is made; but to others [He gives] after the manner of adoption (*secundum adoptionem*), that is, what is from God, namely generation. And thus one God the Father is declared, who is above all, and through all, and in all.[12]

THE SON WHO ESTABLISHED ADAM'S EXISTENCE RE-ESTABLISHES THE HUMAN NATURE

According to the Valentinians, the Savior Aeon was produced by Monogenes as a result of the fall of Sophia, "lest any of the aeons should fall into a calamity similar to that of Sophia" (*AH* 1.2.5). For Irenaeus, the logic was exactly the reverse, since "it was necessary that what might be saved should also be called into existence, in order that the Being who saves should not exist in vain."[13] In fact, the Son not only eternally co-existed with the Father (*AH* 1.30.9), but the Father was creating all things "by the Word" in such a way that the Son's distinct activity of creating is expressed by the bishop thus: "the Word 'establishes', that is, works bodily and confers existence (subsistentiam-existentiae; *huparxis*)"[14] Likewise, he uses a

---

11. *AH* 5.12.2; (SC 153:146). Emphasis mine.
12. *AH* 5.18.2; (SC 153:240).
13. *AH* 3.33.2.
14. *Epid.* 5; (SC 406:90).

The Consummation

similar expression to speak of the Son's own coming as the Second Adam, saying:

> When, however, the Word of God became flesh, He confirmed both these: for He both showed forth the image truly, since He became Himself what was His image; and He *re-established the similitude* (*similitudinem firmans restituit*) after a sure manner, by assimilating man to the invisible Father through means of the visible Word.[15]

Aside from affirming the physical body by sharing the same substance with Adam, the incarnation was eschatologically efficacious for the faithful, because it was about restoring and remaking their human nature.[16] Irenaeus employs the expression "reestablish" to emphasize the continuity of the act of incarnation with the Son's distinct activity of creating Adam. The bishop avers, then, that the eternal Son had healed the broken human nature in his own person through the incarnation.[17] Moreover, in saying, "when He became incarnate, and was made man, He commenced afresh the long line of human beings" (*AH* 3.18.1), he implies that this was for Christ to blaze the trail for the faithful to eventually receive the full restoration at the eschaton. Therefore, the Son's act of incarnation "rendered man living and perfect, receptive of the perfect

---

15. *AH* 5.16.2; (SC 153:146). Emphasis mine.

16. On the basis of the Johannine flesh-to-Spirit Christological vision Andia envisages "the humanity of the Word as more and more grasped by the Spirit until it becomes the source of the gift of the Spirit in glory." (*Homo Vivens*, 186). She adduces as evidence *AH* 3.9.3; 3.17.2–3 and 3.18.7. However, these texts do not necessarily support her view. What Irenaeus says—which might be the closest to her assertion appears in (*AH* 3.20.2): "the Word of God who dwelt in man, and became the Son of man, that He might *accustom* man to receive God, and God to dwell in man, according to the good pleasure of the Father" (*Homo Vivens*, 185). Christ's baptizm have "accustomed" believers to receive God, but no direct evidence seems to suggest that "the Spirit who transforms [Christ's] flesh... makes it incorruptible in glory."

17. Later, Maximus the Confessor fills in the detail on this Irenaean idea of recapitulation, that Christ "restores human nature to itself . . . in that as a man he kept his will calm and not rebelling against nature and did not let it become unsettled in its own movement contrary to nature" (*Or. Dom.* [CCSG 23:34.135–6]).

Father, in order that as in the natural [Adam] we all were dead, so in the spiritual we may all be made alive" (*AH* 5.1.3).

But what of the resurrected human nature among the faithful? But to investigate how Irenaeus says this is achieved we shall now turn to the third and final activity of the Spirit.

THE SPIRIT WHO ARRANGED ADAM'S POWERS REINTEGRATES THEM IN THE RESURRECTION

In describing the Spirit's unique role in creating Adam, Irenaeus perhaps depends on Psalm 32:6 and says, "the Spirit arranges and forms (*aptat-et-format*) the various "powers," so rightly is . . . the Spirit the Wisdom of God."[18] These "various powers" refer to human capacities such as "visual powers" (*AH* 4.20.1; 5.15.3), or "powers of mind, reason, and speech" (*Frag.* 6). As such, we are told that a human being is "a created and organized being" (*AH* 4.38.3), as the Spirit "arranges and forms" these capacities inherent in human nature. In fact, Irenaeus scrupulously says that the Second Adam also received the same "arrangement" belonging to human nature by the Spirit:

> Thus, the Lord, recapitulating this man, received the same *arrangement* (*dispositionem*; *oikonomia*) of embodiment (*carnationis*; *sarkosis*) *as this one*, being born from the Virgin by the will and wisdom of God, that He might also demonstrate the likeness of embodiment to Adam, and might become the man, written in the beginning, "according to the image and likeness of God."[19]

Christ was then anointed with the Spirit at baptism on the behalf of the faithful, so that the Spirit would indwell them from Pentecost thenceforth (*AH* 3.17.2). Irenaeus is aware that two questions remain: (1) How does the Spirit begin to influence those powers in whom he dwells up to the resurrection? and (2) What is

---

18. *Epid.* 5; (SC 406:90). Behr infers that Irenaeus is perhaps following Theophilus since both omit part of the verse Ps 32:6.

19. *Epid.* 32; (SC 406:128).

The Consummation

the significance of those influences when the Spirit finally raises up the human body to reunite it with the soul? The answers anticipate two different kinds of influences of the Spirit—one for progressive sanctification of the soul, and the other for the transformation by means of the Spirit's reintegrating the body, soul, and the Spirit at the final resurrection.

First, with respect to the believers' progressive sanctification, he describes the dynamic function or movement of the soul between the Spirit and the flesh:

> "That flesh and blood cannot inherit the kingdom of God." This is [the passage] which is adduced by all the heretics in support of their folly, with an attempt to annoy us, and to point out that the handiwork of God is not saved. They do not take this fact into consideration, that there are three things out of which, as I have shown, the complete man is composed—flesh, soul, and Spirit. One of these does indeed preserve and fashion [the man]—this is the Spirit; while as to another it is united and formed—that is the flesh; then [comes] that which is between these two—that is the soul, which sometimes indeed, when it follows the Spirit, is raised up by it, but sometimes it sympathizes with the flesh, and falls into carnal lusts.[20]

While his opponents presuppose that Paul was distinguishing immaterial from material substances, Irenaeus points to the functional modes of these substances as well. Thus, while the Spirit's union with the soul and body is significant, Irenaeus also stresses that sanctification or removal of sin's corrupting power in the life of the believer requires the soul's dependence on the leadership of the indwelling Spirit. Moreover, the bishop does not say sin resides in, or emerges from, the body,[21] even though the soul "sometimes

20. *AH* 5.9.1.

21. Irenaeus speaks against his gnostic opponents for embracing Plato's transmigration of souls that added to the theory that evil influence emerged from the body: "The body, therefore, does not cause the soul to forget those things which have been spiritually witnessed; but the soul teaches the body, and shares with it the spiritual vision which it has enjoyed" (*AH* 2.33.3).

sympathizes with the flesh." Instead, he insists that sin rises essentially from a disorderly functional mode or movement of the soul in coordination with respect to the body and the Spirit as a whole. And since the soul sometimes sympathizes with the flesh, sanctification occurs a little at a time, despite the Spirit's presence in the believer.[22]

The remaining question has to do with what the Spirit uniquely does as the final activity of transforming the human nature that includes the resurrection body. In the section where he distinguishes the presence of the Spirit from that of the created breath of God, Irenaeus gives expression to this phenomenon. If disorderly mode of existence between body, soul, and Spirit characterizes the effect of corruption remaining in the believers in this age, it is not surprising why he says this union of body, soul, and the Spirit needs further reintegration at the end:

> If anyone take away the image and set aside the handiwork, he cannot then understand this as being a man, but as either some part of a man, as I have already said, or as something else than a man. . . And for this cause does the apostle, explaining himself, make it clear that the saved man is a complete man as well as a spiritual man; saying thus in the first Epistle to the Thessalonians, "Now the God of peace sanctify you perfect (*perfectos*); and may your spirit, and soul, and body be preserved whole without complaint to the coming of the Lord Jesus Christ." Now what was his object in praying that these three—that is, soul, body, and spirit—might be preserved to the coming of the Lord, unless he was aware of the [future] *reintegration and union of the three* (*redintegrationem et adunitionem trium*), and [that they should be heirs of] one and the same salvation? For this cause also he declares that those are "the perfect" who present unto the Lord the three [component parts] without offense.[23]

---

22. In keeping with his characteristic understanding of progressive human growth, he also maintains that for now we "receive a certain portion of His Spirit," but this is "preparing us for incorruption, being little by little accustomed to receive and bear God" (*AH* 5.8.1).

23. *AH* 5.6.1.

The Consummation

Having contended that the salvation involves the whole human person,[24] constitutive of body, soul, and the Spirit, he describes the nature of the Spirit's work at the resurrection with the phrase "the future reintegration and union of the three." Irenaeus infers here that the resurrected believers at "the coming of the Lord" will no longer neglect the indwelling Spirit, even occasionally; instead, the soul will always function properly in relation to the Spirit and the body, because the soul and the body would also be perfectly coordinated or integrated, always following the Spirit. For this reason, Irenaeus explains the continuity between the old and the resurrected human nature thus: "For it is not one thing which dies and another which is quickened . . . but simply obtained these anew in a healthy condition" (AH 5.3-5). Therefore, the complete transformation required for the resurrection will include reintegration for proper coordination of the soul, the body, and the Spirit.

CONCLUSION

God's breath created, animated, and helped humanity come to senses about life's vulnerability to sin's power to separate body and soul. But God will unite them again through his Son and the Spirit,

---

24. The Valentinians interpreted the phrase "flesh and blood cannot inherit the kingdom of God" (1 Cor. 15:50a), to mean that only our immaterial substance can survive death. See e.g., "The Gospel of Philip", 260-61: "'Flesh and blood shall not inherit the kingdom of God' (1 Cor. 15.50). What is this which will not inherit? This which is upon us." This is drawn most likely from that principle about causation predominant in ancient philosophy including Aristotle, *Physics* 8. 257b 9-10: "it is that which is hot that produces heat, and in general that which produces the form possesses it." Irenaeus explains that the perishable flesh and blood transformed will be able to inherit the kingdom: "Now its transformation [takes place thus], that while it is mortal and corruptible, it becomes immortal and incorruptible, not after its own proper substance, but after the mighty working of the Lord, who is able to invest the mortal with immortality, and the corruptible with incorruption" (AH 5.13.3). Modern New Testament commentators generally agree with Irenaeus that the literal "flesh and blood" will undergo transformation at the Parousia. For example, Fee, *The First Epistle to the Corinthians*.

since his breath was also given to prefigure what God intended for the restless soul and body, beginning with the faithful getting accustomed to the leadership of the Spirit. At last, the faithful will undergo transformation in such a way that even their soul and the body will become perfectly *reintegrated* and made whole, *re-established* in the image and likeness of God. Such will be the end of sin's power, and the faithful will be granted union and communion with the Father through the Son by the Spirit.[25]

In this trinitarian reading of his defense of the resurrection, Irenaeus concentrates on the big picture by telling the overarching narrative of the divine economy. This allows him to suggest a perspective that helps the church in the second century to think about the divine purpose revealed from the beginning of history as being foundational for considering the resurrection possibility. The Son and the Spirit work together inseparably as the Father's two hands, yet he structures the discussion according to the distinct roles and contributions of each member of the Godhead to draw out an effective administration of the divine economy. These distinct roles also reveal the divine purpose that human development should occur in progressive stages. The Father's breath infused into Adam anticipated the last Adam uniting with the Spirit, which union thereby became the model for human beings indwelt by the Spirit.

Conceiving human development in this way, Irenaeus suggests that the three divine acts of union brought forth distinct purposes by each Person, but they were all about achieving humanity's friendship with God, even as such union and communion is exemplified and embodied by the Trinity. And most importantly, Irenaeus insists that the incarnation is not just one of the three events, as it were, but it is crucial not only because Christ recapitulates the broken *imago Dei* by assuming the created nature, but because he becomes the pivotal agent especially for "imparting God to men" by uniting himself with the Spirit. The goodness and power of God, the sacrificial blood redemption of the Son,

---

25. Irenaeus also views numerous resurrections in the canonical books as temporary occurrences signaling what is to come: "that His words concerning its [future] resurrection may also be believed" (*AH* 5.13.1).

and "the complete grace of the Spirit" have a purpose for human destiny that cannot be defeated, and this trinitarian consideration of the divine economy answers to a coherent story that God always intended the renovation of the entire *imago Dei* including the body.

Bibliography

Anatolios, Khaled. *Athanasius: The coherence of his thought*. NY: Routledge, 1998.
Aristotle. *Complete works of Aristotle: The revised Oxford translation*. Edited by J. Barnes. 2 vols. Princeton, NJ: Princeton University Press, 1983.
Augustine. *The Nicene and Post-Nicene Fathers: First Series, Volume II. St. Augustine: City of God, Christian Doctrine*. Peabody, MA: Wm. B. Eerdmans, 1989.
———. *The Trinity*. Vol. 5 of *The Works of Saint Augustine: a Translation for the 21st Century*. Translated by Edmund Hill and John E. Rotelle (Brooklyn, N.Y.: New City Press, 1991
Bacq, Philippe. *De L'ancienne À La Nouvelle Alliance Selon S. Irénée: Unité Du Livre Iv de L'adversus Haereses*. Paris: Lethielleux, 1978.
von Balthasar, Hans Urs. *The Glory of the Lord: a Theological Aesthetics*. Translated by Andrew Louth et al. Edinburgh: T. & T. Clark, 1984.
Barnes, Michel René. "Irenaeus' Trinitarian Theology." *Nova et Vetera*, 7 no. 1(2009) 67–107.
Behr, John, ed., *St. Irenaeus of Lyons: On the Apostolic Preaching*. Crestwood, N.Y.: St Vladimir's Seminary Press, 1997.
Beyschlag, Karlmann. *Simon Magus und die christliche Gnosis*, WUNT 16. Tübingen: Mohr Siebeck, 1974.
Bhabha, Homi K. *The Location of Culture*, London: Routledge, 1994.
Bock, Darrell L. *The Missing Gospels: Unearthing the Truth Behind Alternative Christianities*. Nashville: Thomas Nelson, 2007.
Boyarin, Daniel. *Border Lines: The Partition of Judaeo-Christianity*. Philadelphia: University of Pennsylvania Press, 2004.
Briggman, Anthony. *Irenaeus of Lyons and the Theology of the Holy Spirit*. NY: Oxford University Press, 2012.
Brown, Raymond. *The Epistles of John*. Garden City, N.Y.: Doubleday, 1982.
Cartwright, Sophie. "The Image of God in Irenaeus, Marcellus, and Eustathius." In *Irenaeus: Life, Scripture, Legacy*, edited by Sara Parvis and Paul Foster. Minneapolis: Fortress Press, 2012.

Bibliography

Charlesworth, J. H. "A Critical Comparison of the Dualism in 1QS 3:13-4:26 and the 'Dualism' Contained in the Gospel of John." *New Testament Studies* 15 (1968-69) 389-418.

Daniélou, Jean. *The Theology of Jewish Christianity*. London: Darton, Longman & Todd, 1964.

Davies, J. G. "The Origins of Docetism." In *Studia Patristica* 6, edited by F. L. Cross, 13-35. Berlin: Academie-Verlag 1962.

De Andia, Ysabel. *Homo Vivens. Incomiptibilité et divinisation de l'homme selon Irénée de Lyon*. Paris: Études Augustiniennes, 1986.

Donovan, Mary A. *One Right Reading*. Collegeville, MN: Liturgical, 1997.

Dunn, James D. G. *Neither Jew nor Greek: a Contested Identity*. Vol. 3 of *Christianity in the Making*. Grand Rapids, MI: Eerdmans, 2015.

———. *The New Perspective on Paul Revised Edition*. Grand Rapids, MI: Eerdmans, 2008.

———. "Paul, Grace and *ERGA NOMOU*." In *Ancient Perspectives on Paul*. Edited by T. Nicklas et al., 263-75. Göttingen: De Gruyter, 2013.

———. Review of *Border Lines: The Partition of Judaeo-Christianity*, by Daniel Boyarin. *JTS* 57/1 (April 2006) 338-41.

———. *Romans 9-16, Word Biblical Commentary*. Dallas: Word Books, 1988.

———. *The Theology of Paul the Apostle*. Grand Rapids, MI: Eerdmans, 1998.

Epiphanius. *The Panarion of Epiphanius of Salamis (Book I [Sections 1-46])*. Translated by Frank Williams. Leiden: E. J. Brill, 1987.

Fee, Gordon. *The First Epistle to the Corinthians*, Revised ed. Grand Rapids: Eerdmans, 2014.

Fox, Robin Lane. *Pagans and Christians: In the Mediterranean World from the Second Century AD to the Conversion of Constantine?* New York: HarperCollins, 1988.

Franzmann, Majella. "A Complete History of Early Christianity: Taking the 'Heretics' Seriously." *Journal of Religious History* 29, no. 2 (June 2005) 117-28.

Gathercole, S. J. *Where is Boasting? Early Jewish Soteriology and Paul's Response in Romans 1-5*. Grand Rapids: Eerdmans, 2002.

Goldstein, Ronnie and Guy G. Stroumsa. "The Greek and Jewish Origins of Docetism: A New Proposal." *Zeitschrift Für Antikes Christentum* 10 (March 2007) 423-41.

Greeven, H. "*proskuneo*." In *TDNT* 6:758-60, edited by Gerhard Kittel, G. Bromiley and G. Friedrich. Grand Rapids: Eerdmans, 1964-76.

Gregory of Nyssa, *Ad Ablabium. Quod non sint tres dei*. In GNO III, 1.35-57, edited by Fridericus Mueller. Leiden: Brill, 1958.

Gunton, Colin E. *The Triune Creator*. Edinburgh: Edinburgh University Press, 1998.

Haar, Stephen. *Simon Magus: The First Gnostic?* Berlin: Walter de Gruyter, 2003.

Hill, Charles E. "Cerinthus, Gnostic or Chiliast? A New Solution to an Old Problem." *Journal of Early Christian Studies* 8, no. 2 (2000) 135-72.

Bibliography

———. "The *Epistula Apostolorum*: An Asian Tract from the Time of Polycarp." *Journal of Early Christian Studies* 7 (1999) 1-53.

———. *From the lost teaching of Polycarp: Identifying Irenaeus' apostolic presbyter and the author of Ad Diognetum.* Tübingen: Mohr Siebeck, 2006.

———. "Irenaeus and John, By the Numbers." *The Expository Times* 119/5 (2008) 233.

Hippolytus. *Refutation of All Heresies.* Translated by M. David Litwa, Atlanta: SBL, 2015.

Hoeller, Stephen A. *Ecclesia Gnostica. Collects, Lessons, and Gospels: Lectionary* (2010) 136. http://gnosis.org/ecclesia/Ecclesia-Gnostica-Lectionary.pdf.

Hoeller, Stephan A. and Tau Stephanus I. *The Gnostic Catechism*, http://www.gnosis.org/ecclesia/catechism.htm.

Irenaeus. *The Ante-Nicene Fathers: The Writings of the Fathers Down to A.D. 325 Volume I - The Apostolic Fathers with Justin Martyr and Irenaeus.* Grand Rapids: Eerdmans, 1989.

Irénée de Lyon. *Contre les Hérésies 1.1&2.* SC 263 & 264. Traduction, Introduction, et Notes par Adelin Rousseau & Louis Doutreleau. Paris: Éditions du Cerf, 1979.

Irénée de Lyon. *Contre les Hérésies 2.1&2.* SC 293 & 294. Traduction, Introduction, et Notes par Adelin Rousseau & Louis Doutreleau. Paris: Éditions du Cerf, 1982.

Irénée de Lyon. *Contre les Hérésies 3.1&2.* SC 210 & 211. Traduction, Introduction, et Notes par Adelin Rousseau, et al. Paris: Éditions du Cerf, 1974

Irénée de Lyon. *Contre les Hérésies 4.1&2.* SC 100.1 & 100.2. Traduction, Introduction, et Notes par Adelin Rousseau & Louis Doutreleau. Paris: Éditions du Cerf, 1965.

Irénée de Lyon. *Contre les Hérésies 5.1 &2.* SC 152 & 153. Traduction, Introduction, et Notes par Adelin Rousseau, Louis Doutreleau, & Charles Mercier. Paris: Éditions du Cerf, 1969.

Irénée de Lyon. *Démonstration de la Prédication Apostolique.* SC 406. Traduction, Introduction, et Notes par Adelin Rousseau. Paris: Cerf, 1995.

St Irenaeus of Lyons. *On the Apostolic Preaching.* Translated by John Behr. New York: St. Vladimir's Seminary Press, 1997.

James, Montague Rhode. *The Apocryphal New Testament.* Oxford: Clarendon Press, 1924.

Justin Martyr, *Dialogus cum Tryphone.* Edited by Miroslav Marcovich. PTS 47; Berlin: De Gruyter, 1994.

———. *The First and Second Apologies.* ACW 56. Translated by L. W. Barnard. NY: Paulist, 1997.

King, Karen L. *What is Gnosticism?* Cambridge, MA: The Belknap Press of Harvard University Press, 2003.

Klijn, A. F. J. and G. J. Reinink. "Patristic Evidence for Jewish-Christian Sects." Leiden: Brill, 1973.

Bibliography

Lake, Kirsopp. "The Epistola Apostolorum." *The Harvard Theological Review* 14, no.1 (Jan., 1921) 15-29.
Lampe, G. W. H. *Patristic Greek Lexicon* (Oxford: Clarendon Press, 1961.
Lashier, Jackson *Irenaeus on the Trinity*. Leiden: Brill, 2014.
Layton, Bentley. *The Gnostic Scriptures*. Garden City, NY: Doubleday & Co., 1987.
———. "Prolegomena to the Study of Ancient Gnosticism." In *The Social World of the First Christians: Essays in honor of Wayne Meeks*, edited by Michael White, 334-50. Minneapolis: Fortress, 1995.
Liddell, H. G., Scott, R., Jones, H. S. and R. McKenzie, s.v. "*gnome*." In *A Greek-English Lexicon*, 9th ed. Oxford: Clarendon Press, 1996.
Lüdemann, Gerd. *Heretics. The Other Side of early Christianity*. London: SCM Press, 1996.
Mackenzie, Iain M. *Irenaeus' Demonstrations of the Apostolic Preaching*. Burlington: Ashgate, 2002.
Marcovich, Miroslav. *Dialogus cum Tryphone*. PTS 47; Berlin: De Gruyter, 1994.
Markschies, Christoph. *Gnosis: an Introduction*. New York: T&T Clark, 2003.
Marshall, Steven. "Meditations: Gnostic Homilies," http://www.gnosis.org/ecclesia/homilies.htm.
Maximi Confessoris Opuscula exegetica duo. Greek text edited by Peter van Deun. Vol. 23 of Corpus Christianorum, Series Graeca. Turnhout: Leuven University Press, 1991.
Migne, Jaques Paul, ed. *Patrologia Cursus Completus: Series Graecae*. Vol. 45. Paris: n. p., 1857-66.
Minns, Denis. *Irenaeus: An Introduction*. NY: T&T Clark International, 2010.
Noormann, Rolf. *Irenäus Als Paulusinterpret: Zur Rezeption Und Wirkung der Paulinischen Und Deuteropaulinischen Briefe Im Werk Des Irenäus von Lyon*. Tübingen: Mohr Siebeck, 1994.
Osborn, Eric. *Irenaeus of Lyons*. Cambridge: Cambridge University Press, 2001.
———. *Justin Martyr*. BZHT 47; Tübingen: Mohr, 1973.
Paget, James C. Review of *Border Lines: The Partition of Judaeo-Christianity*, by Daniel Boyarin. *Journal of Jewish Studies* 56/2 (Autumn 2005) 338–41.
Pearson, Birger A. *Gnosticism and Christianity in Roman and Coptic Egypt*. London: T&T Clark, 2004.
Pearson, Birger A. "Early Christianity and Gnosticism in the History of Religions." *Studia Theologica* 55 (2001) 81-106.
Perkins, Pheme. "Identification with the Savior in Coptic Texts from Nag Hammadi." In *The Jewish Roots of Christological Monotheism: Papers from the St. Andrew's Conference on the Historical Origins of the Worship of Jesus*, edited by Carey C. Newman, James R. Davila, Gladys S. Lewis Leiden: Brill, 1999.
Pétrement, Simon. *A Separate God: The Christian Origins of Gnosticism*. Translated by Carol Harrison New York: Harpercollins, 1993.
Prigent, Pierre. *Justin et l'Ancien Testament*. Paris: J. Gabalda & Cie, 1964.

Bibliography

Roberts, Alexander, James Donaldson, and A. Cleveland Coxe, eds. *Ante Nicene Fathers, Volume 1: Apostolic Fathers, Justin Martyr, Irenaeus.* Peabody, MA: Wm. B. Eerdmans, 1989.

Robinson, James M. *The Nag Hammadi Library in English.* 4th ed. New York: Brill Academic Publishers, 1997.

Rokéah, David. *Justin Martyr and the Jews.* Leiden: Brill, 2002.

Runia, David T. *Philo in Early Christian Literature.* Minneapolis: Fortress, 1993.

Schmidt, Carl. *Gespräche Jesu mit seinen Jüngern nach der Auferstehung.* Leipzig: J. C. Hinrichs, 1919.

Skarsaune, Oskar. "Is Christianity Monotheistic? Patristic Perspectives on a Jewish/Christian Debate." In *Studia Patristica 36,* edited by Elizabeth A. Livingstone, 340-63. Leuven: Peeters, 1997.

———. *The Proof from Prophecy.* SNT 56; Leiden: Brill, 1987.

Smith, Geoffrey S. *Valentinian Christianity: Texts and translation,* Oakland, University of California Press, 2020.

Stanton, G. N., Longenecker B. W. and S. C. Barton, eds. *The Holy Spirit and Christian Origins: Essays in Honor of James D. G. Dunn.* Grand Rapids, MI: Eerdmans, 2004.

Stanton, G. N. "The Two Parousias of Christ: Justin Martyr and Matthew." In *From Jesus to John: Essays on Jesus and New Testament Christology in Honour of Marinus de Jonge,* 183-95, edited by M. C. de Boer. Sheffield: JSOT, 1993.

Steenberg, M. C. *Irenaeus on Creation.* Leiden: Brill, 2008.

Stendahl, Krister. *Paul among Jews and Gentiles and Other Essays.* Philadelphia: SCM, 1976.

Stewart-Sykes, A. "The Asian Context of the New Prophecy and of *Epistula Apostolorum.*" *Vigiliae Christianae* 51 (1997) 416-38.

Stylianopoulos, Theodore. *Justin Martyr and the Mosaic Law.* Missoula, MT: Scholars, 1975.

Trakatellis, Demetrius C. *The Pre-existence of Christ in the Writings of Justin Martyr.* Vol. 6 of Harvard Dissertations in Religion. Edited by Caroline Bynum and George Rupp. Missoula: Scholars Press, 1976.

Tremblay, Réal. *La Manifestation Et La Vision de Dieu Selon Saint Irénée de Lyon.* Vol. 41 of *Münsterische Beiträge Zur Theologie.* Münster: Aschendorff, 1978.

Visscher, Gerhard H. *Romans 4 and the New Perspective on Paul: Faith Embraces the Promise.* New York: Peter Lang, 2009.

Watson, Francis. "By Faith (of Christ): An Exegetical dilemma and its Scriptural Solution." In *The Faith of Jesus Christ: Exegetical, Biblical, and Theological Studies,* 147-61. Edited by Michael F. Bird and Preston M. Sprinkle. Peabody, MA: Hendrickson, 2009.

Weiss, H.-F. *Untersuchungen zur Kosmologie des hellenistischen und palästinischen Judentums.* TU 97. Berlin: Akademie-Verlag, 1966.

Bibliography

West, M. L. "Towards Monotheism." In *Pagan Monotheism in Late Antiquity*, edited by Polymnia Athanassiadi et al., 23–24. Oxford: Clarendon Press, 1999.

Wiegel, James B. "The Trinitarian Structure of Irenaeus' *Demonstration of the Apostolic Preaching*." *St Vladimir's Theological Quarterly* 58/2 (2014) 113–139.

Williams, D. H. "Justification by Faith: a Patristic Doctrine." *Journal of Ecclesiastical History* 57/4 (2006) 649–67.

Williams, Michael A. *Rethinking "Gnosticism": An Argument for Dismantling a Dubious Category*. Princeton: Princeton University Press, 1996.

Wisse, Frederik. "The Nag Hammadi Library and the Heresiologists." *Vigiliae Christianae* 25 (1971) 214-16.

Wright, N. T. "The Letter to the Romans." In *Acts, Introduction to Epistolary Literature, Romans, 1 Corinthians*. Vol. 10 of *The New Interpreter's Bible*. Nashville: Abingdon, 2002.

Yinger, Kent L. *The New Perspective on Paul: An Introduction*. Eugene, Oregon: Wipf and Stock, 2011.

www.ingramcontent.com/pod-product-compliance
Lightning Source LLC
Chambersburg PA
CBHW071217160426
43196CB00012B/2334